GEORGE MULLER ON PRAYER

---

31 PRAYER INSIGHTS FOR DEVELOPING AN
INTIMATE RELATIONSHIP WITH GOD

GODLIPRESS TEAM

© Copyright 2023 by GodliPress. All rights reserved.

This book is copyright protected. You cannot amend, distribute, sell, use, quote or paraphrase any part, or the content within this book, without the consent of the author or publisher, except in the case of brief quotations embodied in critical articles or reviews.

Scripture quotations are from The ESV® Bible (The Holy Bible, English Standard Version®), copyright © 2001 by Crossway, a publishing ministry of Good News Publishers. Used by permission. All rights reserved.

CONTENTS

Introduction   vii

1. PRAYING IN SECRET   1
   Daily Reflections   3
2. THE LORD'S PRAYER   5
   Daily Reflections   8
3. THE LORD'S PRAYER (CONTINUED)   10
   Daily Reflections   12
4. OPEN YOUR MOUTH WIDE   13
   Daily Reflections   16
5. A PRAYER-HEARING GOD   17
   Daily Reflections   19
6. CASTING OUR BURDENS ON HIM   21
   Daily Reflections   23
7. STARTING THE DAY   25
   Daily Reflections   28
8. WAITING ON GOD   29
   Daily Reflections   32
9. PRAY WITHOUT CEASING   33
   Daily Reflections   36
10. STRENGTHENING YOUR FAITH FOR PRAYER   37
    Daily Reflections   40
11. THE GIFT OF FAITH IN PRAYER   41
    Daily Reflections   43
12. PRAYING IN FAITH   45
    Daily Reflections   48

13. PRAYER FOR EVERY NEED	49
Trusting Him Alone	50
Daily Reflections	51
14. WHY WE WAIT ON THE LORD	53
Daily Reflections	55
15. THE WORD AND PRAYER	57
Daily Reflections	59
16. KEEPING A PRAYER JOURNAL	60
Daily Reflections	62
17. RISING EARLY	64
Daily Reflections	66
18. PRAYERFULLY READ THE BIBLE	68
Daily Reflections	70
19. PRAYING PRIVATELY FOR NEEDS	71
Daily Reflections	73
20. PROMISES AND ANSWERS	75
Answers to Prayer	76
Praying and Receiving	77
Daily Reflections	78
21. TRUSTING IN HIM FOR ANSWERS	79
Daily Reflections	81
22. PRAYING FOR INTIMACY WITH GOD	83
Daily Reflections	85
23. FAITH IN PRAYING FOR THE SICK	86
Daily Reflections	89
24. WAITING FOR ANSWERS	90
Why We Wait	91
Immediate and Delayed Answers	91
Daily Reflections	93
25. THE POWER OF PRAYING TOGETHER	94
Daily Reflections	96

26. FINDING THE WILL OF GOD	98
Daily Reflections	101
27. EFFECTIVE PRAYER	102
1- Entire dependence on the merits and mediation of Jesus as the only ground for any claim for blessing.	102
2- Separation from all known sin.	103
3- Faith in God's promise, confirmed by His oath.	104
4- Asking in accordance with His will.	104
5- Persistence in supplication.	105
Daily Reflections	105
28. PRAYING TO SHARE THE WORD	107
Daily Reflections	109
29. PRAYING TO SHARE THE WORD (CONTINUED)	110
Daily Reflections	111
30. IN EVERYTHING BY PRAYER	113
Daily Reflections	115
31. CONFIDING IN GOD	117
Daily Reflections	120
More on Prayer	121
About George Muller	123
Bibliography	127

INTRODUCTION

What makes someone a person of great faith? What makes them become someone who is extraordinary in their time that their name is heard and revered? Their words about God become classics, their actions continue as examples, and their lives are testimonies. They are the people we talk of who rise above mere Christianity.

Looking back over the last hundred or so years, there are a number of men and women who stand above the rest as beacons, extraordinary Christians who shone brightly during their time on earth. They are often called men and women of great faith. They seemed to grasp hold of the hem of Jesus' cloak and never let go, drawing as much for their own lives as for those around them.

It was men like these who have become examples to us—those who abandoned to the call of Jesus. We look at them and marvel, wishing we could somehow aspire to the level of spirituality that they did. They lived what they preached. They lived what they believed. George Muller was one such man!

But he differs from those who stand tall in the hall of faith. He is not immediately known for his incredible preaching, although he brought the word of God many times to congregations across the world. He is not well-known for miraculous healings or other amazing acts of God. He is not known for profound writings, bringing deep teachings in many different books.

Mostly, he is known for his work among orphans in Bristol during the late 1800s. But Muller was not content to simply act out his Christian faith by doing good for homeless children. He did not want to let good works get in the way of showing the world what a miraculous, faithful God he served. He wanted his orphanages to be living illustrations of what God can do when you trust him in prayer.

Muller was a man of prayer! His whole life was built around his time with God, bringing everything before the Lord; requests, petitions, and problems. Nothing was too small for him to trust that God would hear and provide an answer. Muller never asked anyone for anything, except God.

This is his legacy. He wrote detailed narratives of his daily life, the struggles he faced opening orphanages and schools, his dependence on the Lord to provide for them all, and the incredible answers he received. We have included many of these extracts, complete with the dates, so you can see and read about his dealings with God when it came to prayer.

We have also included some of his sermons and explanations of the Bible and what they say about prayer. There is no greater way to learn about prayer than from someone who practiced it every day, personally, seeing answers to his requests almost daily. Muller was simple and straightforward, cutting straight to the heart of the matter. He did not use incredibly descriptive phrases or clever analogies and stories to show us, he used his own life as a clear example. The way he lived speaks for itself!

The hours he spent in prayer, the way he learned to pray, and the knowledge he gained from these times with the Lord are all recorded for our benefit. Muller never saw himself as a great man of anything. He knew he was a sinner saved by grace and prayer was a privilege given so that he could commune with God. He knew he was an ordinary man having a spiritual encounter with the Almighty! And he believed each one of us can have that same experience.

Taking the best of his narratives, sermons, and writings, we have put them together in this collection. In the format of a 31-day devotional, we have brought forward his most inspiring and encouraging words, which are as true and pertinent today as they were back then. We have kept the heart of what he wrote over a hundred years ago, only altering and adjusting any phrases to make it easier for us in this modern era to understand. In addition, we have included daily reflections at the end of each chapter. These are not to distract or add any further meaning to what Muller says, but rather to give you a chance to think through the words and reflect on them for your own life.

As part of our series on prayer, this book about Muller's life stands out for its simplicity and detailed accounts of what can happen when you bring faith and prayer together. It is an encouragement for each one of us about the exciting and wonderful things we can expect when we begin to put such aspects into action in our own lives.

> "The joy that comes from answers to prayer, cannot be described, and the energy they bring to the spiritual life is exceedingly great."

1
PRAYING IN SECRET

"But when you pray, go into your room and shut the door and pray to your Father who is in secret. And your Father who sees in secret will reward you"
Matthew 6:6

Let us look at Matthew 6, starting at verse 5: *"And when you pray, you must not be like the hypocrites. For they love to stand and pray in the synagogues and at the street corners, that they may be seen by others."* The Pharisees would stand for a long time in the synagogues praying, but worse than this, when the ordinary prayer time came for the Israelites—about three o'clock in the afternoon—they could be found on the corners of the streets, where they might be seen in the act of prayer by as many as possible. All this was hypocrisy. They professed to be holy men, but in reality, it was the opposite. *"Truly, I say to you, they have received their reward."* Their reward was the applause of others. A poor, miserable reward.

"But when you pray, go into your room." The main point here is the secrecy in prayer. Not everyone has a little room where they can go and lock the door. But if it can be done, it should be done. If impossible, God will accept your circumstances. I went to Germany to find missionaries for the East Indies and came to Magdeburg where I found a soldier who was a believer. I said, "How do you manage with prayer since you are continually surrounded by hundreds of soldiers?" His reply was, "When I want to pray in secret, I go down into a large cellar, which is perfectly dark, and there I kneel down on the sand. No one is able to see I am there, though often some of my comrades come close, but never find me. I am alone, perfectly alone. No one sees me, and that is my closet."

So, in whatever circumstances, Christians have to do the best they can. But the main point is that as much as possible we should look to deal with our Heavenly Father in secret prayer. Under no circumstances try to be noticed by others to get their applause.

"But when you pray, go into your room and shut the door and pray to your Father who is in secret. And your Father who sees in secret will reward you." When you are secretly waiting on God, in His own time and way, He will reward you. He will show that He is noticing. He will show that He has recorded it in the book of remembrance. He will show that it has not escaped His observation. The secret waiting on God will be revealed by blessing. As we pray, God will notice us, and bless us in a way others will be able to see.

"And when you pray, do not heap up empty phrases as the Gentiles do" (v. 7). Sentence by sentence, repeating the same request, just as Baal's worshippers did, and as the pagans do, thinking that more words, the more times they ask, the more they will get it. *"For they think that they will be heard for their many words. Do not be like them, for your Father knows what you need before you ask him"* (v. 7-8). Prayer is not necessary to inform God, but prayer is necessary simply because it is the appointment of God. He wants us to go to Him for our own good, profit, and blessing, asking Him for the things we need, because the blessing given to us in answer to prayer is much more precious than if the blessing were given without prayer.

Often God allows us to be tested so that at last, when the blessing does come and prayer is answered, it may be more precious to us.

Daily Reflections

These reflections are designed to deepen your understanding of Muller's words. By asking questions for you to answer, they will make you think about the verses used, the words written, and what God is trying to say to you. Some of the questions may be personal—our spiritual walk and growth is a personal one. So, don't be shy or too quick to skip over those questions, as they will show you where you need to change things to allow God to work.

1. Why does Jesus make praying in secret such a big deal?

2. What kind of reward is waiting for those who pray publicly for others to see?
3. What kind of reward is there for those who pray privately to God?
4. How often do you pray on your own, without anyone seeing or knowing about it? Is it difficult for you?
5. Why do we often think the more words we use, the more we will be heard?

2
THE LORD'S PRAYER

"Pray then like this: *Our Father in heaven, hallowed be your name. Your kingdom come, your will be done, on earth as it is in heaven. Give us this day our daily bread*"
Matthew 6:9-11

"*Pray then like this:*" This shows us it is not God's intention that these words of Jesus are the only ones to be used, nor that we should always use them. But in the spirit, in this way we ask. That is the lesson we have to learn.

"*Our Father in heaven.*" The requests are only for the children of God, those who are believers in Jesus. If we are not believers in Jesus, God is not our Father. God is God to us. He is our Creator. He is our Preserver. He is the One Who supplies us with everything that we need. He lets His sun shine for us. He lets the rain fall so that we benefit from it. But until we are believers in Jesus, God is not our Father.

Now the word *"our"* shows that we are part of a family, part of the heavenly family. Everyone who puts their trust in Jesus for the salvation of their souls, after being convinced that they are sinners, deserving nothing but punishment, has a Father in God Almighty. The phrase *"in heaven"* shows His place is everywhere but especially in heaven, not on earth, though His power can be seen everywhere, and the evidence of His presence can be found throughout the universe.

"Hallowed by your name." Your name is honored, Your name is glorified. The meaning of the word "name" does not mean the letters making up the name of God, but what we learn in Exodus 34 when Jehovah proclaimed His name before Moses. It is His character, His attributes, and what He is, that is to be glorified. Jehovah, the God and Father of Jesus, the Father of all those who believe in Jesus, is to be glorified. And as we enter into what God is, we find out what a lovely being He is, how infinitely lovely He is. In other words, "I pray that You may be more and more honored and glorified."

Now, comes another request. *"Your kingdom come."* Make it happen soon when You are universally honored and glorified, when all the works of the wicked one are destroyed. This will be after the return of Jesus. See how impossible it is for the ungodly, the unconverted, to ask this from the heart. Their lips may say it many times, but the true meaning is: "Let the time come soon when I, a wicked person, will be thrown into the bottomless pit."

The words can only properly be used by those who are believers in Jesus because they beg Him to return soon, so that God may be glorified and honored by everyone on earth.

We can see this from the words that follow. *"Your will be done, on earth as it is in heaven."* Since the fall of Adam and Eve, the will of God is not done on earth. It was done before the fall, but from the moment they ate of the forbidden fruit, and sin was introduced by the devil on earth, from that moment the will of God was not done on earth as it should be, and as it will once Jesus has returned. One of the first things after the fall was that Cain murdered his own brother, Abel, the fruit of sin entered into the world, and ever since then the will of God has not been *"done on earth, as it is in heaven."*

"Give us this day our daily bread." Here the daily bread does not simply mean bread and nothing else. It means the general necessities of life. What we need we ask God for, and are allowed to ask God to give to us. Notice that it does not say "Give us our daily bread," but *"Give us this day our daily bread."* That means we are not to expect a great abundance of earthly things. God may fill our hearts with reasons for gratitude, He may abundantly give to us the necessities of life. But if He does not, we are not to blame Him, or think He is not faithful to His promise, for He has not promised that He will give us years, months, weeks, or days before we need. He has only promised that day by day we shall be supplied, and only if we seek first the Kingdom of God and His Righteousness.

In other words, if we walk in the fear of God, trying to win souls for Him and setting a good example before others, as we trust in Him, we will be given the necessities of life. David said, *"I have been young, and now am old, yet I have not seen the righteous forsaken or his children begging for bread"* (Psalm 37:25).

"Give us this day our daily bread." On this request, we can write clothes, rent, taxes, and supplies for everything our family requires. How incredible to go to a Loving Father, whose joy and delight it is to answer the requests of His children. He is not a hard master, an aloof being, but an infinitely loving Father. If we as Christians just see Him as an infinitely loving Being, we will be in an attitude where we are perfectly satisfied at all times and under all circumstances with His dealings with us. Whether painful or otherwise, we are satisfied that He does everything well.

Daily Reflections

There are not many people who do not know the Lord's Prayer or at least know a part of it. This is partly because it has been overdone, repeated too many times, and said without meaning. It has become a set of words to ramble off in religious institutions or at ceremonies rather than a personal cry from our hearts. And yet, the meaning Jesus wanted to teach us is very clear as we look at each verse on its own.

1. Do you ever pray the Lord's Prayer? In what context and why?
2. Have you ever tried using the format but using your own words instead to bring a more personal meaning?
3. Why is it important to begin by acknowledging who God is to us?

4. Why does Muller say the words "kingdom come" and "will be done" can only really be prayed by born-again Christians?
5. Do you really believe God can meet all your needs, every single one?

3

THE LORD'S PRAYER (CONTINUED)

> *"And forgive us our debts, as we also have forgiven our debtors.*
> *And lead us not into temptation,*
> *but deliver us from evil"*
> Matthew 6:12-13

"**F**orgive us our debts, as we also have forgiven our debtors." If anyone has offended us, transgressed against us, or behaved improperly toward us, are we ready to forgive? Are we habitually forgiving? Even if it should happen many times, and the person who offends us confesses, we are to be ready to forgive. We should not expect answers to our prayers if we are not acting according to this. This is often a hindrance to obtaining answers to our prayers because we have an unforgiving spirit, we are not ready to forgive those who have offended us.

"And lead us not into temptation." Our weakness and helplessness stay with us. As long as we are in the body, we will have temptation and be exposed to it. Jesus experienced this. The tempter may leave us alone, not looking to overpower us, but it will be only for a season, he will come again. The other side of the truth is that God is ready to support and help His children. All through our journey, if we own our weakness and come to Him and look for His assistance, He is ready to help. Our prayer should be that God, in His grace, would allow us not to be tempted more than necessary for the glory of His Name, so we can become more and more aware of His power, love, and readiness to appear on our behalf.

Then it says, *"but deliver us from evil."* That means the devil himself, because he is the source of evil and is continually trying to take advantage of us. So, our prayer should be: "Deliver us from the wicked one, the devil; allow him not to take advantage of us." We never become so perfectly holy, so perfectly sinless, so perfectly Christ-like, that the devil can never take advantage of us. I never trust myself, I admit my own weakness and helplessness to God and continually cry to Him to keep me from the craftiness and deceit of the wicked one because if I was left to myself, regardless of how long I have walked in God's ways, my life would end just as Asa's did. For 30 years he glorified God, but in the last two years of his life, he dishonored God. So, because of my own weakness, my prayer is always, "Lord, allow me to finish my journey with joy and not to bring shame and dishonor to Your Holy Name."

"For thine is the kingdom, and the power, and the glory, for ever. Amen" (Matt. 6:13 KJV). These words show us the "Why" to

expect answers to our prayers. The Kingdom is the Lord's, He is able to do it. He is the Mighty One, the Powerful One. This is further confirmed by the word *"Amen."* Yes! So it shall be. In this evil world, we can encourage ourselves with this statement. It is wonderful that we do not speak into the air, but that we speak to the loving heart of God Almighty, who can do everything and who is willing on behalf of His children to do everything that is for their real blessing in Christ.

Daily Reflections

When we look at the Lord's Prayer with an open mind, removed from the religious format it has become, we can see Jesus' intention in using it as a teaching tool. The meaning behind the words becomes clear to us. It is a personal prayer where we rely on God for everything while recognizing who we are and who God is in the process. Instead of a ritualistic invocation, it is a very intimate intercession between us as children of God and our Father in heaven.

1. Forgiveness is very prominent in the prayer, why do you think this is?
2. Temptation is also integral here. Why is it so important to ask God every day for help in this area?
3. What is the difference between not being led into temptation and being delivered from evil?
4. Why can we expect God to answer our prayers?
5. Do you ever say "Amen" at the end of a prayer? Why?

4

OPEN YOUR MOUTH WIDE

"I am the LORD your God, who brought you up out of the land of Egypt. Open your mouth wide, and I will fill it"
Psalm 81:10

During the first two weeks when I began thinking about establishing an orphanage, I only prayed that if it was of the Lord, he would bring it about, but if not, then He would take all thoughts about it out of my mind. My uncertainty about knowing the Lord's mind did not come from questioning whether it would be pleasing in His sight, that there should be a home and a place of Scriptural education to provide for homeless children without parents; but whether it was His will that I should be the instrument of making it happen, as my hands were already more than filled. My comfort was that if it was His will, He would not only provide the means but also suitable individuals to take care of the children so that my part of the work would take only so much of my time to not conflict with my many other engagements. The whole of those two weeks I never asked the Lord for money or for people to engage in the work.

On December 5th, 1835, however, the subject of my prayer changed. I was reading Psalm 81 and was struck with verse 10: *"Open your mouth wide, and I will fill it."* I thought about these words for a few moments and then was led to apply them to the case of the orphanage. It struck me that I had never asked the Lord for anything concerning it, except to know His will.

I fell on my knees and opened my mouth wide, asking Him for much. I asked in submission to His will, and without fixing a time when He should answer my request. I prayed that He would give me a house, either as a loan, that someone might be led to pay the rent for one, or that one might be given permanently for this project. I also asked Him for £1,000, and for suitable individuals to take care of the children. Besides this, I had also been led to ask the Lord to put into the hearts of His people to send me furniture for the house and some clothes for the children. When I was asking this, I was fully aware of what I was doing—that I was asking for something which I had no natural prospect of obtaining from those I know, but which was not too much for the Lord to give.

Are you weak and sick in your body, suffering pain? This verse applies to you, *"Open your mouth wide, and I will fill it."* With our business, career, or profession, are there specific trials or difficulties? Humbly, quietly, gently bring it before God and leave it there. This is the very best remedy! Not just in physical matters, but in spiritual things, too. In our spiritual conflict, there is nothing better than to remember this wonderful promise, *"Open your mouth wide, and I will fill it."* We feel the natural evil tendencies within us, we struggle against them, we seek to overcome them, and we find ourselves too weak, but God is able to help us, and out of these things He will bring us.

It encourages us to come to God and ask great blessings for these things, and we will find how ready He is to help us so that pride, carelessness, and laziness, indulgence in natural sinful ways, can be overcome by the power of the Holy Spirit.

"Open your mouth wide, and I will fill it." It does not say, "Perhaps I will fill it," or "I will see if I will do it or not." He does not say, "If you are doing so and so, I will fill it." We do not have to fill our mouths after we have opened them wide. We do not have to fulfill the promise in our own power, ability, and skillfulness. We leave this to God. He will do it. We do not have to look to others to bring about the answer to prayer, as we often do. We look to others, instead of having our eyes fixed on the almighty power and the loving heart of God. *"I will fill it,"* He says. We do not have to look to circumstances, or a contingency in everyday things and affairs, but our eyes must be focused on God Himself. *"I will fill it."*

We do not have to be discouraged because our mouth is not immediately filled. We do not have to be discouraged because the answer does not come immediately. Know that in connection with all the many hundreds of promises given to us in connection with prayer, in the Old and New Testaments, there is not one single passage to be found where

God makes a statement in connection with this promise regarding the time when He will fulfill it. He simply states everywhere, "I will do it," "I will answer it." He never says, "At such a time I will answer," or "At such a time I will fill your mouth." But He simply states "I will do it."

Daily Reflections

It is a good idea to use a notebook as you work through these readings and daily reflections. If a verse or a phrase sticks out to you, write it down. If Muller's words leap out at you, copy them into the book. Keeping a record of your own answers to the questions is also helpful, as you can revisit them. It is a waste to read, move on, and forget, as we all often do. To be able to come back to certain issues the Lord wants to highlight in our prayer lives is an important part of allowing Him to show us spiritual things.

1. What was the difference in the way Muller was praying before he read the verse and after?
2. What does it mean to open our mouths wide?
3. "Submission to His will" is an important part of prayer. Why?
4. What do you understand by the words *"I will fill it"*?
5. Do you find it hard to pray in such a direct way, expecting God to fulfill His promise?

5

A PRAYER-HEARING GOD

*"And this is the confidence that we have toward him,
that if we ask anything according to his will he hears us.
And if we know that he hears us in whatever we ask,
we know that we have the requests that we have asked of him"*
1 John 5:14-15

If we pray and want our requests to be granted, we must first see to it that we ask for things according to his will. Our blessing and happiness are intimately connected with the holiness of God. Imagine there was a lazy person who did not like working, and he heard of the promises about prayer. If he said, "Now I will see if this is true, and I will ask God to give me lots of money, and then I can travel and enjoy myself." Imagine he prays every day for this money, will he get it? Definitely not! Why not? He does not ask for it that he may help the poor or contribute to the work of God, but he asks that he can spend his life enjoying the pleasures of the world. He is not asking for things according to the mind of God, and therefore, however long or sincerely he prays, he will not get the answer. We are only guaranteed in expecting our prayers to be answered when we ask for things according to the mind of God.

We must see that we do not ask on account of our own goodness or merit but in the name of Jesus. *"Whatever you ask in my name, this I will do, that the Father may be glorified in the Son. If you ask me anything in my name, I will do it"* (John 14:13-14). The statement is said twice to show the importance of this truth. It means that if we want to go to Heaven, how will we get there? Because of our own goodness? Because we are not as bad as others? Because we regularly go to church? Because we give to the poor? The best person in the whole world is a sinner deserving of punishment. No one since the fall of Adam has by his own goodness gotten to heaven. A sinner only gets to heaven by faith in Jesus for the salvation of his soul.

If we want our requests answered, we must not come in our own name, but as sinners who trust in Jesus, who by faith in His name are united in the risen Lord. We cannot think we are good enough. We deserve nothing but hell.

But Jesus is worthy, and for His sake, our prayers are answered. There is nothing too great for God to give to Him. He is worthy. And if we trust in Him, if we hide in Him, if we put Him forward and ourselves in the background, depend on Him, and plead His name, we can expect to have our prayers answered. If you say, "I have prayed for my children, but they have not yet been born again. I feel I shall not have my prayers answered. I am so unworthy," this is a mistake. The promises are for the weak, ignorant, and needy. All who ask in Jesus' name can expect their prayers to be answered.

But if we live in sin, the prayer cannot be answered, because it says in Psalm 66:18, *"If I had cherished iniquity in my heart, the Lord would not have listened."* If I live in sin and carry on against God, I cannot expect my prayers to be answered.

We must have faith in the power and willingness of God to answer our prayers. This is very important. In Mark 11:24, we read, *"Therefore I tell you, whatever you ask in prayer, believe that you have received it, and it will be yours."* I have found in the 54 years of being a believer, that if I only believed, then I was sure to get the thing I asked for in God's time. I emphasize that you must have faith in the power and willingness of God to answer your requests. We must believe that God is able and willing. To see that He is able, you have only to look at the resurrection of Jesus, because having raised Him from the dead, He must have almighty power. Regarding the love of God, you only have to look at the cross and see His love in not sparing His Son, in not holding back His only Son from death. With these proofs of the power and love of God, then if we believe, we shall receive—we will obtain.

Daily Reflections

This seems as though it should be common sense—God hears us. Often, we pray wondering if anyone really is listening, whether He doesn't have something better to do than hear our concerns and issues. But when we realize He is a prayer-hearing God, no matter how trivial, His ear is attentive to our hearts. Knowing this, believing this, will change the way we bring our requests and petitions to Him. If He hears, then surely He will answer us as well.

1. Do you believe God hears you 100% of the time?
2. Why is it important to line our prayers up with His will?
3. Do you ever view God in a Santa Claus way, where you feel you deserve an answer because you have been good? How is this contrary to the way God works?
4. When does God not listen to us?
5. What do you understand by the word *"whatever"* in Mark 11:24?

6

CASTING OUR BURDENS ON HIM

"Ask, and it will be given to you; seek, and you will find; knock, and it will be opened to you. For everyone who asks receives, and the one who seeks finds, and to the one who knocks it will be opened."
Matthew 7:7-8

Our heavenly Father knows where we are as we pass through this evil world. All the trials, difficulties, confusing circumstances, and temptations we are exposed to, He is intimately acquainted with. For that reason, His word is full of promises so that we should be encouraged to roll our burdens on Him. It is not His will that we should carry them in our own strength, but speak to Him about everything, walk with Him continually, and so roll all our burdens on Him. He does not just invite us to do this, but He advises us, He encourages us, to do so. I can even say that He commands us to do so, in order that we may find ease and comfort in our trials and difficulties. It is because we do not make use of our God that we so often find things so difficult in this world. If we habitually rolled our burdens on the Lord, our position would be a hundred times better than it is.

Are you in the habit of rolling all your burdens on the Lord? Just as trials come, do you bring them back to your heavenly Father? This is the reason why He lays them on you. And if you try to carry them in your own strength, you will oblige your heavenly Father to increase the trial and burden, so that by the weight you may be at last forced to come to Him, and leave it with Him. Then again, Jesus has passed through hardships, and *"has been tempted as we are, yet without sin"* (Heb. 4:15). All His temptations came from outside, none from within, because He was the spotless One. But He was still tested, going through many incredible difficulties. And He knew how it would happen with us who would be left in this world, and so His love led Him to make this provision for us, that by prayer we should bring the burden back to Him.

Now, let me ask you Christians, do you take the advice of Jesus? And do you believe what He says when He speaks in the verse, *"Ask, and it will be given to you; seek, and you will find; knock, and it will be opened to you"* (Matt. 7:7)? Let us take it to our hearts! I believe He wants us to understand what these words literally convey to us. *"For everyone who asks receives, and the one who seeks finds, and to the one who knocks it will be opened"* (Matt. 7:8).

But as wide, broad, and deep as these promises are, they must be taken in context with other portions of Scripture.

We must compare Scripture with Scripture because again and again, we find that one part supplies another with what is needed.

By the grace of God, my heart is not worried, whether we have lots or only a little. I am sure that in the right time and way, God will send help. When boys need to be trained, or situations have to be found for the girls, and there are difficulties, my heart is at peace because I bring myself to my Heavenly Father. When there have been infectious diseases in the orphanages, and it looks as though many children could die, my heart is at peace, because I cast this burden on the Lord, and He sustains me.

I have rolled my burdens on the Lord, and He has carried them for me. The result of that has been that *"peace of God, which surpasses all understanding"* (Phil. 4:7) has kept my heart and mind. If we are worried, it brings about a depressed look, and that dishonors God and puts non-Christians off from seeking the Lord, because they will say, "That person is just as miserable as I am when I am in trouble." But when they see we are in a difficult trial but there we have a cheerfulness, it is an encouragement to them, and also encourages other Christians. We cannot have this peace by our own resolutions by saying to ourselves, "I will go through this bravely." In our weakness and helplessness, we must roll our burdens on God, then we will have the peace of God.

Daily Reflections

This is a tough world, there is no disputing that fact. Jesus told His disciples it would not be easy and they would face trials just like we do today. But He also reminded them of His grace and how they didn't have to carry the weight of every hardship and problem on their own. It's the same for us. He is willing to carry it all for us, if only we will ask Him to, and allow Him to.

1. Just as Muller asks, "Are you in the habit of rolling all your burdens on the Lord?"
2. Do you trust that God can carry every problem and issue, no matter how big or small?
3. Read 1 Peter 5:6-7. What does this mean?
4. Why is a depressing attitude dishonoring to God?
5. What do you understand by the *"peace that passes all understanding"*?

7
STARTING THE DAY

"I rise before dawn and cry for help; I hope in your words."
Psalm 119:147

While I was staying at Nailsworth, the Lord taught me a truth, the benefit of which I have not lost, though it's been more than 40 years.

The point is this: I saw more clearly than ever that the main business I should attend to every day was to have my soul happy in the Lord. The first thing to be concerned about was not how much I might serve the Lord or how I might glorify the Lord, but how I might get my soul into a happy state, and how my inner man might be nourished.

I can try telling the truth to those not yet born again, I can encourage believers, I can try to help those in trouble, I can do other things to behave like a Christian in this world; and yet, not being happy in the Lord, and not being nourished and strengthened in my inner man every day, means all this might not be done in the right spirit.

Before Nailsworth, my habit for 10 years had been to pray once I had dressed in the morning. Now, I saw that the most important thing I had to do was to read the Word of God and meditate on it, so my heart might be comforted, encouraged, warned, reproved, and instructed. In meditation, my heart might be brought into communion with the Lord. I began, therefore, to meditate on the New Testament from the beginning, early in the morning.

The first thing I did, after asking for the Lord's blessing on His precious Word, was to begin to meditate on the Bible; searching into every verse to find a blessing, not for ministry of the Word, not for preaching on what I had meditated on, but for obtaining food for my own soul. The result was that after a few minutes, my soul was led to confession, or thanksgiving, or intercession, or supplication, so that even though I was not there to pray but to meditate, yet it turned almost immediately to prayer.

When I had finished making confession, or intercession, or supplication, or given thanks, I went on to the next words or verse, turning everything as I went on into prayer for myself or others, as the Word led me to do so. But I still focused on the food for my own soul as the object of meditation. The result of this is that there is always a good deal of confession, thanksgiving, supplication, or intercession mixed with my meditation, that my inner man almost always is even fed and strengthened, and that by breakfast time, my heart is peaceful and happy. So, the Lord showed me that it is food for every believer. It is not for ministering the Word that we meditate, but for the profit of our inner man.

The difference between the way I used to start the day and the way I do now is this: Before, when I awoke, I began to pray as soon as possible, and generally spent all my time until breakfast in prayer, or almost all the time. I almost always began with prayer... But what was the result? I often spent a quarter of an hour, half an hour, or even an hour on my knees before being conscious of gaining any comfort, encouragement, humbling of the soul, etc. Often, after my mind wandered for the first 10 minutes, or a quarter of an hour, or even half an hour, I only then began to really pray.

Now, I hardly ever suffer in this way. My heart is nourished by the truth, being brought into close fellowship with God. I speak to my Father, and to my Friend (even though I am sinful and unworthy of it!) about the things that He has brought before me in His precious Word. I am still astonished that I did not see this sooner. I never read about it in any book. No ministry ever showed it to me. No discussion with another Christian brought this matter up. And yet now, since God has taught me this point, it is as plain to me as anything that the first thing a Christian has to do every morning is get food for his inner man.

As the physical outer body is not able to work for a long time unless we eat food as we do first thing in the morning, so it should be with our inner man. We should take food for that. Now, what is the food for the inner man? Not prayer, but the Word of God. Not simple reading of the Bible, so that it only passes through our minds, just as water runs through a pipe, but considering what we read, pondering over it, and applying it to our hearts.

I stress this point because of the incredible spiritual profit and refreshment I have found for myself, and I encourage all my Christians to think about it. This method has given me help and strength from God to have peace through deep trials in more ways than I had ever had before. After having done this for 40 years, I fully commend it. How different it is when the soul is refreshed and made happy early in the morning, from being spiritually unprepared for the service, trials, and temptations of the day that lie ahead!

Daily Reflections

It's encouraging to see that even a great man of faith like Muller had to learn how to pray the right way. We are never too young, old, or too spiritual to learn lessons from the Lord. To have an example like this before us and be given the chance to grow is a huge benefit in our Christian walk.

1. What is the first thing you do in the morning? Do you feel you need to change anything?
2. Does your mind ever wander and take time before focusing on the business of praying?
3. Why is the combination of the Bible and prayer so beneficial?
4. Read Psalm 19:14. What does this verse mean?

8

WAITING ON GOD

"Be still before the LORD and wait patiently for him"
Psalm 37:7

If we walk in the fear of God and do not allow anything contrary to the will of God in us, then there remains one thing more—that we continue to wait on God until the answer comes. But we so often break down. We begin well, but we do not go on. If, month after month and year after year, we have been praying, and if our petitions have not been granted, we wonder if God will answer. Many break down because the petition is not granted as quickly as they expected. Parents pray for their children. They begin to do so, but we should never forget that what we have to do is just to continue, day after day, week after week, month after month, and year after year until the answer comes. For God knows the best time for us, and He will, in His own time, give us our requests. It may be for the trial of our faith, or of our patience, or to see if we are sincere, that He waits. For these and other reasons the petitions may not be answered as quickly as we desire.

Young evangelists ask God for the conversion of many souls. They go on praying and preaching, but do not get the answers. It may be that they are not prepared for the blessing. If their petitions were granted, it might be an injury to their souls. Therefore, He waits until they are prepared to receive the blessing. So it is with those who teach our children in our churches. They ask God for good things for their children yet do not receive the answer. Now let us go on and patiently, quietly, wait on the Lord. The blessing most assuredly will come.

Now, are we all in the habit of going on patiently, perseveringly, month after month and year after year, waiting on God? Then let us set out with renewed sincerity and faith. To all our petitions, as they have been according to the will of God and in the name of Jesus, believe in the willingness of God to give what we have asked, that the answers must come.

I have had to wait for a long time to get certain blessings. Many times the answer has come immediately, or in the same hour, or the same day; yet other times I have had to wait years—10 years, 15 years, 20 years, and more—yet the answer has always come. And I say it to encourage Christians, "Go on waiting, waiting, waiting." Begin afresh to bring your petitions before God. He will hear you.

I have been praying for 39 years and 9 months for one specific thing, and the answer has not yet come. Last evening, I prayed for it, and the evening before that I prayed again. When traveling in India and America, year after year I have been praying, and I am sure that in the end, the answer will come. I have received tens of thousands of answers to prayer; but in this particular one, I have to wait.

I prayed for a believer's parents that they might be converted. At last, the answer came when the father was between 80 and 90 years old. He had cut off his son entirely; for years he did not allow him to come into his presence. At last, he sent for him, and then would hardly let him go, but I had to pray for his conversion for 20 years. It was the same with the mother. She had lived a very moral life outwardly, very hypocritically, but at last, she saw that nothing but Jesus would do for her, and she was saved.

Therefore, we must begin afresh with more sincerity than before, and we will eventually receive the answers. The Lord delights to bless His children, to give us everything that is for our blessing and comfort; and He especially delights to bless parents praying for their children. But if we have set them a bad example, should we have let them go on in a self-willed course? Then the first thing is to make an honest confession of our sin and failure, that we deserve all these things that come upon us. We must humble ourselves in the dust before God, pleading the merits of Jesus, and we will find that God is always ready in His pity and compassion to forgive us. Then, with renewed earnestness, let us begin to pray.

My universal remedy for every difficulty, for every trial, is prayer and faith. And in this way, for 55 years I have been going on. I desire to encourage Christians who have not tried this universal remedy, and they will find, as I have, that it suits every difficulty and trial.

Daily Reflections

We need the Holy Spirit as we read through these daily passages. He is the counselor and teacher who will guide us in all things. And if we want to learn and be taught the things of God, then we must listen and be attentive to the Holy Spirit who will show us. It may be in a single sentence or even a verse we've read so many times before that comes alive with new meaning. Instead of just reading for knowledge, be sensitive to the Spirit's leading.

1. Have you ever waited a long time for something specific in prayer? Did you continue until you received an answer, or did you give up?
2. Why is it so hard to wait on the Lord?
3. Read Psalm 40:1. How does it say we should wait?
4. Read Romans 8:25. Again we find patience and waiting are linked. Are you able to wait like this?
5. What is Muller's universal remedy for every single issue?

9

PRAY WITHOUT CEASING

"Rejoice always, pray without ceasing, give thanks in all circumstances; for this is the will of God in Christ Jesus for you"
1 Thessalonians 5:16-18

We read in Acts 12:3-19 the story of Peter being thrown in prison and his miraculous escape. When he was thrown in jail, the disciples did not say, "Now we will send a petition to Herod to let him go." They could have sent one in because by this time, there were thousands in Jerusalem who believed in Jesus. They were a formidable company by that time. And if they had all written down their names on this petition, they might have succeeded. And if they did not succeed, they might have raised a large sum of money. They were very willing to give what they had and sell their houses and lands for the poor of the church. And most certainly they would have willingly done this for the deliverance of Peter.

They did not do this, even though they could have bribed some of Herod's courtiers to get Peter delivered, since this is what happened in those days. But they did none of these things. They gave themselves to prayer. And that is the best weapon they could have used. There isn't a more wonderful and powerful weapon for Christians than to give themselves to prayer. In this way, they can have the power of God on their side—the almighty power of God. And by making use of this power, through the instrumentality of prayer in all things we need, we can have the infinite wisdom of God working for us, and have God Himself at our side, as children of God.

So, we should make better use of prayer than we have ever done. And you Christians who are in the habit of meeting together often at prayer meetings, expect great things from the hands of God. Look out for miraculous blessings, and you will see how ready He is to give those things which we ask for. This is what these believers in Jerusalem did—they gave themselves to prayer without ceasing. They believed that even though Herod had captured Peter in order to kill him, and even though Herod was a notoriously wicked man, God was still able to deliver him from this bloodthirsty king. They believed that nothing was too hard for God to accomplish, and therefore, they prayed without ceasing.

Now, we do not know how long Peter was in prison, but it is logical that he had been taken before those days of unleavened bread. His execution was to take place after this time, which means he was in prison for at least seven days. It was not on the first day that the prayer was answered. They met together and prayed—prayed sincerely, but the first day, hour by hour, passed away, and Peter was still in prison. The second day came, and again, they were found waiting on God in prayer. Still, hour by hour, the second day passed, and he was not delivered. And so the third, and fourth, and fifth days went by. They were still waiting on God. Prayer happens without ceasing, but this holy man remained in prison. There seemed to be no prospect of God answering their prayers.

You and I will also find again and again that the answer is delayed. The question we ask is, "Shall we give up praying, or shall we continue?" The temptation is to cease praying, as though we had given up hope, and to say, "It is useless, we have already prayed so long that it is useless to continue." This is just what Satan wants us to say, but let us persevere and go on praying, and be confident that God is both able and willing to do it for us. That it is the joy and delight of His heart, for Jesus' sake, to give to us all things which are for the glory of His name, and our benefit. If we do so, He will give us what we desire. Since we are children of God, if we pray perseveringly and in faith, the prayer will be answered.

"By prayer and supplication" (Phil. 4:6). Ordinary prayer and repetitious prayer is not enough. We must ask in the same way a beggar asks for coins, chasing us down the road and not letting us go until something is given to him. In this way, we have to bring our matters before God in order to have the blessing. And notice that this is to be done "with thanksgiving." We have to lay a good foundation with praise and thanksgiving, and then build on this prayer and supplication for whatever our position in life, however huge or different our trials and hardships might be.

Daily Reflections

Never giving up is crucial if we want to see breakthroughs in our Christian lives. If we want to see our prayers answered, we need to continue, despite the circumstances. Here we see the church so busy praying for Peter's release, they almost miss the fact that the answer is knocking at their door!

1. Their first option is to pray. Is this your natural choice when facing an issue, or do you try other things first?
2. Why is prayer called a "powerful weapon"?
3. What does it mean to "give yourself to prayer"?
4. Why does Satan want to discourage us from continuing in prayer?
5. Read Luke 18:1-8. Are you anything like the widow in the story when it comes to praying?

10

STRENGTHENING YOUR FAITH FOR PRAYER

"The testing of your faith produces steadfastness. And let steadfastness have its full effect, that you may be perfect and complete, lacking in nothing"
James 1:3-4

You might ask, "How can I have my faith strengthened?" The answer is this:

"Every good gift and every perfect gift is from above, coming down from the Father of lights, with whom there is no variation or shadow due to change" (James 1:17). As the increase of faith is a good gift, it must come from God, and therefore, He should be asked for this blessing.

However, the following should be used:

Careful reading of the Bible with meditation. Through this, the believer becomes more acquainted with the nature and character of God—besides His holiness and justice, what a kind, loving, gracious, merciful, mighty, wise, and faithful Being He is. We will rely on the willingness of God to help us because we have not only learned from the Scriptures what a kind, good, merciful, gracious, and faithful being God is but because we have also seen in the Word of God how He has proved Himself to be so. If God has become known to us through prayer and meditation on His Word, we will be led with a measure of confidence to rely upon Him. Reading the Word of God, together with meditation, will be one way to strengthen our faith.

How can I possibly continue to have faith in God, for anything, if I am habitually grieving Him, detracting from the glory and honor of Him in whom I say I trust, on whom I say I depend? All my confidence toward God, all my leaning on Him in the hour of trial, will be gone if I have a guilty conscience and continue to do things that are contrary to the mind of God. If I cannot trust in God because of a guilty conscience, then my faith is weakened by that mistrust. Faith with every fresh trial either increases by trusting God or decreases by not trusting him. Then there is less and less power of looking simply and directly to Him, and a habit of self-dependence grows and is encouraged.

Either we trust in God, and so neither trust in ourselves, in others, in circumstances, nor anything else; or we *do* trust in one or more of these, and in that case do *not* trust in God.

If we desire our faith to be strengthened, we should not shrink from opportunities where our faith may be tried and strengthened. In our natural state, we dislike dealing with

God alone. This sticks with us, even after being born again. Even as believers, we have the same shrinking from standing with God alone—from depending on Him alone, from looking to Him alone—and yet this is the very place we should be if we want our faith to be strengthened. The more I am in a position to be tried in faith with my body, my family, my service to the Lord, my business, etc., the more I shall have the opportunity of seeing God's help and deliverance. Every fresh instance in which He helps and delivers me will increase my faith.

So, the believer should not shrink from situations, positions, or circumstances in which his faith may be tried but should cheerfully embrace them as opportunities where he may see the hand of God stretched out on his behalf, to help and deliver him, and have his faith strengthened.

The last important point for the strengthening of our faith is that we let God work for us when the trial of our faith comes, and do not deliver ourselves. Wherever God has given faith, it is for the very purpose of being tested. However weak our faith may be, God will test it. Now, when the trial of faith comes, we are naturally inclined to distrust God and to rather trust in ourselves, in our friends, or circumstances.

We will rather make a plan of our own than simply look to God and wait for His help. But if we do not patiently wait for God's help, our faith will decrease. But, where we stand still to see the salvation of God, to see His hand stretched out on our behalf, trusting in Him alone, then our faith is increased.

If we want our faith strengthened, we must give time to God, who tries our faith in order to prove to His child, in the end, how willing He is to help and deliver us.

Daily Reflections

Faith is an integral part of the Christian life. Without it, we are left with meaningless rituals. Prayer is just a lot of useless words spoken to the air without faith. And so, we need to grow in faith if we want to become spiritual men and women of God. Muller gives us practical steps for how we can go about strengthening our faith and allowing God to build us up in this area.

1. Have you ever asked God to increase your faith?
2. What is faith? Read Hebrews 11:1 and see if your answer matched up with this verse.
3. Why is the Bible an important part of growing in faith?
4. Why is self-dependence counteractive to faith?
5. How often do you think of making your own plan rather than trusting the Lord? Why?

11

THE GIFT OF FAITH IN PRAYER

"And whatever you ask in prayer, you will receive, if you have faith"
Matthew 21:22

I want all who read this to increase in more simple confidence in God for everything which you may need in any circumstances, and that these answers to prayer may encourage you to pray, especially as it regards the conversion of your friends and family, your own progress in grace and knowledge, the state of the Christians whom you know personally, the state of the church, and the success of the preaching of the Gospel.

I want to warn you against being led away by the schemes of Satan, thinking that these things are only applicable to me and cannot be enjoyed by all Christians. Every believer is not called to establish orphanages, charity schools, etc., or to trust in the Lord for them. But all believers are called in the simple confidence of faith to cast all their burdens on Him, to trust in Him for everything, and not only to make everything a subject of prayer but to expect answers to requests which have been asked according to His will, and in the name of Jesus.

Do not think that I have the gift of faith which we read about in 1 Cor. 12:9, and which is mentioned along with the gifts of healing, the working of miracles, and prophecy, and because of that, I am able to trust in the Lord. It is true that the faith I have is God's own gift. It is true that He alone supports it, and that He alone can increase it. It is true that, moment by moment, I depend on Him for it, and that if I were left to myself, my faith would completely fail. But it is not true that my faith is that gift of faith which is spoken of in 1 Cor. 12:9 for the following reasons:

The faith which I have when it comes to the orphanages and my own physical needs is not that faith in 1 Cor. 13:2: *"If I have all faith, so as to remove mountains, but have not love, I am nothing."* It is the same faith that is found in every believer, and the growth which I see, little and little, has been increasing in me for the last 69 years.

This faith which is exercised for the orphanages and my own physical needs shows itself in the same measure concerning the following: I have never doubted during the last 69 years that my sins are forgiven, that I am a child of God, that I am beloved of God, and that I shall be finally saved. I am enabled, by the grace of God, to exercise faith in the word of

God, and believe what God says in those passages which settle these matters (1 John 5:1, Gal. 3:26, Acts 10:43, Romans 10:9-10, John 3:16, etc.)

When natural circumstances have seemed very dark and troubling in connection to my ministry among Christians, when I should have been overwhelmed with grief and despair by looking at everything around me; at such times, I have encouraged myself in God by holding onto His mighty power, His unchangeable love, and His infinite wisdom in faith, and I have said to myself: "God is able and willing to deliver me, if it is good for me." It is written: *"He who did not spare his own Son but gave him up for us all, how will he not also with him graciously give us all things?"* (Rom. 8:32). This is what I believed through grace, and it kept my soul in peace.

Daily Reflections

As Christians, the word faith is mentioned and dropped into conversations and sermons so often that it loses its potency and meaning. Just like love, there is much more to it than an attitude of heart or an addition to our lifestyle. Muller's intention is to make sure we understand that the faith he exhibited is available to each one of us. It's not something out of our reach—we can all have faith to move mountains.

1. Read Matthew 17:20. What does this verse mean? Is it applicable to all Christians?
2. What is the gift of faith spoken of in 1 Corinthians 12:9? How is it different from normal faith?

3. How would you rate your faith on a score out of 10?
4. Do you have faith for what you pray for? How do you know?

12

PRAYING IN FAITH

*"And without faith it is impossible to please him,
for whoever would draw near to God must believe
that he exists and that he rewards those who seek him"*
Hebrews 11:6

When dealing with the orphanages, day schools, etc., trials have come on me which were far heavier than I could bear. When false reports were spread that the orphans did not have enough to eat or that they were cruelly treated; or when other bigger trials happened in connection with this work, and I was almost a thousand miles away for a number of weeks; at such times my soul focused on God.

I believed His word of promise which was true in every circumstance. I poured out my heart before God and got up from my knees in peace, because the trouble that was in the heart was placed on God in believing prayer, and I was kept in peace, even though I saw it was the will of God for me to remain far away from the work. When I needed houses, fellow workers, masters, and mistresses for the orphans or the day schools, I was able to look to the Lord and trust in Him for help in everything.

I may seem to boast, but by the grace of God, I do not boast about what I am saying. From my heart, I credit God alone for enabling me to trust in Him. He has not betrayed my confidence in Him to fail. But I thought it necessary to make these remarks so that no one should think that my dependence on God was a special gift given to me, which other Christians have no right to look for. I say it so no one should think that my dependence on Him was only for obtaining *money* by prayer and faith.

By the grace of God, I desire that my faith in God should extend toward *everything*: from the smallest of my own physical and spiritual concerns, and the smallest of the physical and spiritual concerns of my family, toward the Christians among whom I work, the church, etc.

Do not think that I have gained such a degree of faith to which I might and should attain, but thank God for the faith which He has given me, and ask Him to uphold and increase it. Do not let Satan deceive you by making you think that you could not have the same faith and that it is only for people like myself.

When I lose a key, I ask the Lord to direct me to it, and I look for an answer to my prayer. When a person with whom I have made an appointment does not come according to the agreed time and I begin to be inconvenienced by it, I ask the

Lord to hurry him to me and I look for an answer. When I do not understand a passage in the Bible, I lift up my heart to the Lord, by His Holy Spirit, He would instruct me, and I expect to be taught, though I do not dictate the time and the manner of how it should be. When I am going to minister in the Word, I look for help from the Lord, even though I know my natural inability and unworthiness to do His service, I am not depressed, but happy, because I look for His assistance and believe that He will help me.

In my other physical and spiritual concerns, I pray to the Lord and expect an answer to my requests. Can you not do the same, dear believing reader? I encourage you not to think of me as an extraordinary believer, having privileges above other Christians which they cannot have. Do not look at how I behave as something that would not do for other believers. Try it for yourself! Stand still in the hour of trial, and you will see the help of God if you trust in Him. But so often we leave the ways of the Lord in the hour of trial, and the food of faith —the way our faith can be increased—is lost.

True faith is when we begin in faith, continue in faith, and are not surprised when the answer comes. If you have children who are not born again living in America, Australia, or New Zealand, for whom you have been praying a long time, and at last you get a letter stating that they have come to the Lord, the test, whether you have been praying in faith or not, is if you react by saying, "The Lord be praised for it" and you accept the news gladly. Then you have been exercising faith. But if you begin to question whether it is real, can it be the case? Then, you know you have not been exercising faith, you have not been expecting your request to be granted.

It's the same as when we use the well-known phrase, "We take it as a matter of course." In a spiritual sense, we should be so confident that God will bless us and that He will answer us in prayer for what we ask that when it comes, can say, "We take it as a matter of course. It could not be any other way. It was always going to happen, because God has promised Himself, in Jesus' name, to give the blessing."

Daily Reflections

Muller carries on speaking about faith since it is one of the foundational truths he lived on and demonstrated—trusting God for everything. He is adamant that we can also have the same faith, believing what we ask for will happen. It's not a motivational claim that we have to take hold of whatever we want, but in line with His will, we can trust He will accomplish it.

1. Why does Muller credit God for enabling Him to trust Him?
2. Why does he specify that he did not just use faith to get money?
3. Why should we not be surprised when God answers our prayers?
4. Is this not an arrogant approach to praying? What is the difference between arrogance and confidence?
5. Read Ephesians 3:12 and comment on this.

13

PRAYER FOR EVERY NEED

"Truly, truly, I say to you, whatever you ask of the Father in my name, he will give it to you"
John 16:23

Many people think that the way we live off donations must lead us to always think about where the food, clothes, etc., will come from, and so make us unsuitable for spiritual exercises. Firstly, our minds are not worried about the necessities of life, because they are laid on our Father, who, because we are His children, not only allows us to wait on Him but wants us to wait on Him. Secondly, it must be remembered that even if we were worrying about the supplies for the children, and the means for the other work, because we look to the Lord for these things, we are brought by our sense of need into the presence of our Father, for Him to supply it. That is a blessing and not an offense to the soul.

Thirdly, our souls realize that for the glory of God and the benefit of the church, we have these trials of faith, and that leads again to God, to ask Him for fresh supplies of grace, to be able to be faithful in this service.

Every Christian is not called by the Lord to establish schools and orphanages, or to trust in the Lord for them, but there is nothing to stop you from knowing, even more than we do now, His willingness to answer your prayers.

Prove the faithfulness of God. Bring every need to Him. All you must do is maintain a pure heart. If you live in sin, if you willfully and habitually do things knowing that they are contrary to the will of God, then you cannot expect to be heard by Him. *"If I had cherished iniquity in my heart, the Lord would not have listened. But truly God has listened; he has attended to the voice of my prayer"* (Psalm 66:18-19).

Trusting Him Alone

Faith rests on the written Word of God, but there is no promise that He will pay our debts. The Bible says, *"Owe no one anything"* (Rom. 13:8). The promise is given to His children, *"I will never leave you nor forsake you"* (Heb. 13:5). *"Whoever believes in him will not be put to shame"* (1 Peter 2:6). We have no scriptural grounds to go into debt.

Our goal is to show the world and the church that even in these evil days, God is ready to help, comfort, and answer the prayers of those who trust in Him. We do not need to go to others or the ways of the world. God is able and willing to supply us with all we need in His service.

We consider it our privilege to continue to wait on the Lord alone instead of buying goods on credit or borrowing money from kind friends. As God gives us grace, we will look to Him only, although we have to depend on Him from meal to meal. God has been feeding these orphans for 10 years, and He has never allowed them to go hungry. He will care for them in the future also.

I am deeply aware of my own helplessness and dependence on the Lord. Through the grace of God, my soul is in peace, although we have to wait on the Lord for our daily bread day after day.

Daily Reflections

Simply reading through this book is good, but it will not bring you spiritual understanding. Read and pray. Ask God to highlight passages, to teach, to illuminate verses for you. He will not show us unless we ask. He is waiting to reveal many treasures to us if only we will come to Him and ask. As you work through the reflections, don't just answer but meditate on them, and allow Him to show you His heart.

1. Why does Muller say his mind was not worried about daily necessities?
2. Even if we do worry, how can we stay in a place of faith and prayer as Muller did?
3. Why is a pure heart so important to have our prayers answered?
4. Why do you think Muller never asked for money or borrowed from anyone?

5. Being "deeply aware of my own helplessness and dependence on the Lord" was critical for Muller. How does this attitude change our prayers?

14

WHY WE WAIT ON THE LORD

"Be still before the LORD and wait patiently for him"
Psalm 37:7

The main reason for our work was not the physical welfare of the children, nor even their spiritual welfare (even though we seek and pray for it). The main reason for the work was to show the whole world and the whole church that even in these last evil days, the living God is ready to prove Himself as the living God by always being willing to help, comfort, and answer the prayers of those who trust in Him. This is so that we do not have to go away from Him to others or the world because He is able and willing to supply us with all we need in His service.

From the beginning, when God put this service into my heart, I had anticipated trials and hardships; but knowing and experiencing the heart of God over several years, I also knew that He would listen to the prayers of His child who trusts in Him and that He would not leave me in the time of need but listen to my prayers and deliver me out of difficulty. When these accounts were published for the benefit of both believers and unbelievers to read about, they would be led to trust in the Lord.

These accounts that I write about are all of the Lord. So, it is for the church's benefit that we are put into these hardships. If in the time of need, we were to take goods on credit, the main reason for our work would be completely undone, and no heart would be encouraged to trust in God. There would also not be any more demonstration of the special provision of God, which has been so evident through this work, even in the eyes of unbelievers, who can see that there is a reality in the things of God. Many of those who read these accounts have been born again as a result.

For these reasons, we consider it our special privilege to continue to wait on the Lord, and no one else, instead of taking goods on credit or borrowing money from some kind friends when we are in need. As God gives us grace, we look to Him only, though morning after morning we have nothing in our hands to continue the work—even though from meal to meal we should have to look to Him. We are fully assured that He, who has been feeding these orphans for 10 years, and who has never disappointed them in what they need and is now carrying on the other parts of our work for 12 years without stopping because we have run out of supplies, will also continue for the future.

Being aware of my natural helplessness and my dependence on the Lord, I will say that through the grace of God my heart has been at peace, though day after day we have had to wait for our daily provisions from the Lord, even though we have had to do this from meal to meal.

Some people begin well, continue well, yet fail completely in the end. They had faith to start and exercised faith, but had no faith in the end. That is what we must avoid. It is easy for us to start well and continue, day after day, week after week, month after month; but it is difficult to stay faithful to the end. We continue outwardly to wait on God, but in the end, we have no more expectations. If we had continued in faith, we would have said, "Blessed the Lord, praise His name!" It should be like this if we are waiting to the end for the blessing, and if it is not, it is proof that faith is gone.

Daily Reflections

Muller is very clear about his mandate for opening the orphanages and schools. Where most people would have been led by humanitarian impulses, he had a much larger vision of using the work of social welfare to bring God glory. It tested him every day and made him dependent on the Lord and His timing and provision. Muller never wavered, even when the answers did not come for a long time.

1. Why does God allow us to wait for Him, sometimes for a long time?
2. Muller says, "as God gives us grace." Why is grace so important when we need to wait?

3. Why do many people fail in the end?
4. Have you waited on God for something for a long time? What was your experience during this?
5. How is expectation linked with faith? Why is it so important when we wait?

15

THE WORD AND PRAYER

"I will meditate on your precepts and fix my eyes on your ways"
Psalm 119:15

God stepped down to become an author of the Bible that His Holy Spirit caused to be written through His servants. It contains everything I need to know, and the knowledge of this will lead me to true happiness. Therefore, I should read this precious book again and again, this book of books, sincerely, prayerfully, and with meditation. In this way, I should continue all the days of my life.

Even though I did not read it much, I was aware that I knew hardly anything about the Bible. But, instead of acting on this to study the Word of God, my ignorance, my difficulty in understanding it, and the little enjoyment I had in it made me careless of reading it (because prayerful reading of the Bible does not just bring more knowledge but increases our delight in reading it). So, like many believers, for the first four years as a Christian, I preferred the works of uninspired men to the oracles of the living God.

The consequence was that I remained a child, both in knowledge and grace. In knowledge, because all true knowledge can only come by the Spirit, from the Word. And as I neglected the Bible, I was ignorant for nearly four years so that I did not even know the fundamental points of our holy faith properly. And this lack of knowledge sadly kept me back from walking steadily in the ways of God.

When the Lord really brought me to the Scriptures in August 1829, my life and spiritual walk became very different. And even though I have still fallen short of what I might and should be, yet by the grace of God I have been enabled to live much nearer to Him than before. If any believers prefer other books to the Holy Scriptures, and who enjoy the writings of men much more than the Word of God, may they be warned by my loss. I pray my testimony will lead some Christians not to neglect the Holy Scriptures any longer but to give them that preference that they have given to the writings of men.

Let me add that if we understand very little of the Word of God, we should read it a lot because the Spirit explains the Word by the Word. And if we only enjoy reading the Word a little bit, that is the reason why we should read it a lot. Frequent reading of the Scriptures creates a delight in us, so the more we read them, the more we desire to do so. Above all, we should want to have it settled in our own mind that God alone, by His Spirit, can teach us. As God will be asked for blessings, it will become natural for us to look for God's blessing before we read, and also while reading.

We should know in our minds that although the Holy Spirit is the best and sufficient Teacher, this Teacher does not always teach immediately when we desire it, and we may have to ask Him again and again for the explanation of certain passages. He will always eventually teach if we are seeking for light prayerfully, patiently, and with a view to the glory of God.

Daily Reflections

Muller was a strong advocate of the Bible. He did not see any way we could pray, have faith, and continue as Christians without the Word of God. You will notice he often links the Bible with prayer, emphasizing an inseparable bond between the two. In his experience, Muller found the combination was a powerful catalyst for growth and consistency in his walk as a Christian.

1. Do you believe God "wrote" the Bible? Why is this significant?
2. What is Muller's view of other books in comparison to the Bible? What impact did they have on his life?
3. Why does he say we should read the Bible a lot?
4. Why is the Holy Spirit so important when it comes to reading the Bible?
5. Why is prayer important when reading the Scriptures?

16

KEEPING A PRAYER JOURNAL

"Bless the LORD, O my soul,
and all that is within me,
bless his holy name!
Bless the LORD, O my soul,
and forget not all his benefits"
Psalm 103:1-2

I believe God has heard my prayers. In His own good time, he will show that He has heard me. I have recorded my petitions so that when God has answered them, His name will be glorified.

I have found it a great blessing to remember all of the answers God graciously gives me. I have always kept a record to strengthen my memory. I advise others to keep a little notebook. On one side—maybe the left-hand side—write down the request and the date when you first brought it to

God. Leave the opposite page blank to put down the answer for each case, and you will soon see how many answers you get, and in this way, you will be encouraged. It will strengthen your faith as you will see what a lovely, generous, and gracious God we have. Your heart will reach out more and more in love to God, and you will say, "It is my Heavenly Father who has been so kind. I will trust in Him, I will confide in Him."

In reading my personal journal, I see that the Lord has given me many wonderful answers to prayer:

One of the orphans needed to be apprenticed. I knew no one who would take an in-door apprentice. I prayed about it every day. I wrote it down among the other things I was asking from the Lord, and after three months of praying, the Lord granted my request. I found a suitable place for the boy.

On May 23rd, I began to ask the Lord to deliver a lady from spiritual depression, and after three days, He granted me my request.

On June 15th, I also began to ask the Lord daily to keep a lady from insanity. After four years, I can now record that the Lord has kept her from it.

On May 25th, I began to ask the Lord for more spiritual prosperity among the Christians whom I work with in Bristol. Now, I can write down and record that He has answered this request, because there has never been more grace and truth and spiritual power among us, than there is while I am writing this.

November 29th, the Lord has blessed our prayer meetings. The proof of all we have received in answer has been recorded.

On many pages you can see an account of how the Lord supplied us with everything in answer to prayers. With every example and proof of how the Lord supplied us, it is to encourage you to see that God, the living God, who has the hearts of everyone in His hands, supplied all this in answer to prayer. If we keep a record in this spirit, and not just for amusement, the result will be that a rich blessing will come to our hearts. This is why we need to record the Lord's unbounded kindness and faithfulness to us.

The joy that comes from answers to prayer cannot be described. The motivation which they bring to our spiritual lives is huge. I want all Christians to experience this joy. If you believe in Jesus for the salvation of your soul, if you walk uprightly and do not allow sin in your heart, if you continue to wait patiently, believing in God; then answers will certainly be given to your prayers. You may not be called to serve the Lord in the way I do, but in your own circumstances, family, business, work, and your efforts for the Lord, you may have answers like those I have recorded.

Daily Reflections

George Muller did not write many books on different topics, delving into spiritual matters. Instead, he kept a meticulous record called *Narratives,* in which he detailed everything that happened during his years running the orphanages. Mostly, these contain things he was praying for and a record of the answers he received from the Lord. He found it to be a great encouragement to have written proof that God does answer prayers.

1. Read 2 Kings 22, the story of Josiah finding the book of law. Why did reading the accounts of God have such an effect on the king?
2. Why was it important for everything to be written down as part of the Bible?
3. What is the benefit of keeping a record of prayers and their outcomes?
4. Have you ever used a notebook in the way Muller describes? If not, why not try it out and see what happens?

17

RISING EARLY

"And rising very early in the morning, while it was still dark, he departed and went out to a desolate place, and there he prayed."
Mark 1:35

I want to encourage all believers to get into the habit of rising early to meet with God. How much time should be given to sleep? No universal rule can be given because people do not all require the same amount of sleep. Also, people, at different times, according to the strength or weakness of their body, may require more or less. Most doctors agree that healthy men do not need more than six or seven hours of sleep, and females need no more than seven or eight hours.

Christians should be careful not to allow themselves too little sleep, since few people can do with less than six hours of sleep and still be well in their body and mind. As a young man, before I went to the university, I went to bed regularly at ten and rose at four, studied hard, and was in good health. Since I have allowed myself only about seven hours, I have been much better in my body and nerves than when I spent eight or eight and a half hours in bed.

Someone may ask, "But why should I get up early?" To stay too long in bed is a waste of time. Wasting time is inappropriate for a believer who is bought by the precious blood of Jesus. Our time and all we have is to be used for the Lord. If we sleep more than is necessary for the refreshment of the body, it is wasting the time the Lord has entrusted us to be used for His glory for our own benefit, and for the benefit of Christians and unbelievers around us.

Just as too much food is bad for the body, the same is true with sleep. Medical experts agree that lying longer in bed than is necessary to strengthen the body actually weakens it. It also injures the soul. Lying too long in bed does not just stop us from giving the most precious part of the day to prayer and meditation, but this laziness also leads to many other evils. Anyone who spends one, two, or three hours in prayer and meditation before breakfast will soon discover the beneficial effect early rising has on the physical and spiritual man.

You might say, "But how do I go about rising early?" My advice is: Do not delay. Begin tomorrow. But do not depend on your own strength. You may have begun to rise early in the past but have given it up. If you depend on your own strength in this, it will come to nothing. In every good work, we must depend on the Lord. If anyone rises so that he may give the time that he takes from sleep to prayer and meditation, let him be sure that Satan will try to put obstacles in the way. Trust in the Lord for help. You will honor Him if you expect help from Him in this matter. Pray for help, expect help, and you will have it. In addition, go to bed early. If you stay up late, you cannot rise early. Let no pressure of engagements keep you from habitually going to bed early. If you fail in this, you won't be able to get up early because your body needs rest.

Get up immediately once you are awake. Do not stay a minute longer in bed or else you are likely to fall asleep again. Do not be discouraged by feeling drowsy and tired from rising early. This will soon wear off. After a few days, you will feel stronger and fresher than when you used to lie an hour or two longer than you needed. Always allow yourself the same hours of sleep. Make no change except when you are sick.

Daily Reflections

Muller is very practical here about the benefits of getting up early to pray. Some of us are not naturally morning people, and yet there is a constant theme of rising early and praying that we can see in many of the great men of faith in the Bible, even Jesus. Seeking God for the day ahead is important if we want to experience His grace and see His hand at work in our lives.

1. Are you a morning person? Do you find it easy to get up early to pray?

2. Why do you think sleep is an issue for many of us when it comes to praying?
3. Why does Muller say wasting time is inappropriate for a believer?
4. Read Psalm 119:147. Why do you think it specifically mentions "before dawn"?
5. What are the physical and spiritual advantages of getting up early?

18

PRAYERFULLY READ THE BIBLE

"All Scripture is breathed out by God and profitable for teaching, for reproof, for correction, and for training in righteousness"
2 Timothy 3:16

We should read the Bible prayerfully, never thinking that we are clever enough or wise enough to understand God's Word through our own wisdom. In all our reading of the Scriptures, let us seek carefully to have the help of the Holy Spirit. Let us ask Him to enlighten us—He is willing to do it.

I will tell you how it was with me when I first started doing this. It might encourage you. It was in 1829 when I was living in Hackney. I had been listening to the teaching on the Spirit by an experienced Christian. "Well," I said, "I will try this plan; and will start with careful reading and meditation of the word of God after prayer, and I will see how much the Spirit is willing to teach me in this way."

I went to my room, locked my door, put the Bible on a chair, and I went down on my knees. I stayed there for several hours in prayer and meditation over the Word of God, and I can tell you that I learned more in those three hours which I spent in this way than I had learned for many months previously. I found the blessing was so great, that all the notes which I had written down from the lectures of the professors in the university that I had attended, I now considered of so little value that when I moved to Devonshire, I did not take them with me. This was because I now found the Holy Spirit to be a better teacher than the professors of theology. I obtained the teaching of the Spirit, and I cannot tell you the incredible blessing it was to my own soul. I was praying in the Spirit and putting my trust in the power of the Spirit as I had never done before.

It should not surprise you, then, that I am stressing this to you when you have heard how precious it was to my heart, and how much it helped me.

We also need to meditate on the Word. It is not enough to only have prayerful reading, but we must also meditate on the Bible. As in the example I just mentioned about kneeling next to the chair, I meditated on the Word; not simply reading it, not simply praying over it. I did all that, but I also pondered over and thought about what I had read. This is very important. If you just read the Bible and nothing else, it is just like water running in one side and out the other. In order to really benefit from it, we must meditate on it.

Not all of us, of course, can spend many hours, or even one or two hours, each day like this. Our business demands our attention. However much time you can afford, give it regularly to reading, prayer, and meditation over the Word, and you will find it will be repaid well.

Daily Reflections

Having your Bible close by as you read through these passages and work through the questions is a real advantage. Not only can you look up verses that are mentioned, but you will be able to find ones that come to your mind as you're reading or others you may see mentioned in the margins of your Bible. Write these verses down, and look them up again later. In this way, you can study the Scriptures on certain points even more, allowing God to teach you.

1. Why shouldn't we read the Bible with our own wisdom?
2. How does prayer help when reading the Bible?
3. How does the Holy Spirit teach us as we read the Scriptures?
4. What is the difference between prayerfully reading the Bible and meditating on it?
5. Why are regular prayer and regular Bible reading important?

19

PRAYING PRIVATELY FOR NEEDS

"Ask, and you will receive, that your joy may be full"
John 16:24

Let us look at the Lord's well-timed help. Why does this bank transfer not come a few days sooner or later? Because the Lord wants to help us through it, and so He influences the donor to send it at that moment, not sooner or later. Surely, all of us who know the Lord can see His hand moving like this in a miraculous way. We cannot say, "There is no difference between doing things like this, or going from individual to individual and asking them for help."

There is a great difference.

Suppose we are in need. Suppose our poverty lasts for weeks or even months. Isn't there a difference between asking the Lord every day, without speaking to any human being not connected directly with what we are facing, and on the other hand, writing letters or making personal applications to people for assistance? There is a great difference between these two methods. I do not mean it goes against the Lord to look for help in His work by personal and individual application to believers (though it would be in direct opposition to His will to apply to unbelievers; 2 Cor. 6:14-18).

I act this way for the benefit of the church, joyfully bearing the trials connected with this life of faith (which brings its own precious joys) if other believers might be led to see the reality of only dealing with God—there is such a thing as Christians having power with God by prayer and faith. That the Lord should use a person so sinful, so unfaithful, so unworthy as me, I can only ascribe to the riches of His grace, in which He uses the most unlikely instruments, that the honor may be all His.

Perhaps the matter of what we are praying for is made known to others (as it was rumored that I prayed publicly for the Lord to send help for the orphans, which is entirely false). To anyone who says I made our requests public, I would ask: Whom did I ask for anything all these years since the work has been going on? To whom did I make our wants known, except to those who are closely connected with the work?

Instead of making our needs known to influence generous people to contribute to the needs of the institution under my care, I have refused to let our circumstances be known, even after having been asked about them when we could have had considerable sums if I had spoken up. I refused, in order that the hand of God might be shown. That is my main aim, not the money, nor the ability to continue the work. The Lord has given me such assurance that at the times of deepest poverty (when we had nothing, and even had to wait on the Lord from meal to meal for over 100 people), when a donation was given to me, the donors could not have read in my face whether we had much or nothing at all.

Hundreds of times we have started the day without money, but our Heavenly Father has sent supplies the moment they were required. There was never a time when we did not have a meal. During all these years I have been enabled to trust in the living God alone. In answer to prayer, $7,500,000 has been sent to me. We have needed as much as $200,000 in one year, and it has all come when needed. No one can ever say I asked them for money. We have no committees, no collectors, no voting, and no endowment. Everything has come in answer to believing prayer. God has many ways of moving the hearts of people all over the world to help us. While I am praying, He speaks to one on this continent and on that to send us help. Only the other evening, while I was preaching, someone wrote a check for a large amount and handed it to me when the service was over.

I have written this so that you should not lose out on the blessing which might come to your heart reading about the Lord's faithfulness and readiness to hear the prayers of His children.

Daily Reflections

Every one of us has been, will be, or is in need—it's part of life. God takes it upon Himself to provide for our basic needs in whatever way He thinks is best. All we need to do is ask. Sometimes we have to approach people we know to get assistance, sometimes we go about asking in a public way so that others might also be aware and be able to help us. Muller took it a step further by testing his own faith and God's generosity—he asked no one but God!

1. Have you ever asked God for something without letting anyone else know your needs? What happened?
2. Why do you think Muller warns against asking unbelievers for help? Do you agree?
3. What was Muller's aim in praying to God alone for every necessity?
4. What does the phrase "believing prayer" mean?
5. Have you experienced the "Lord's faithfulness and readiness to hear the prayers of His children"?

20

PROMISES AND ANSWERS

*"For all the promises of God find their Yes in him.
That is why it is through him that we utter our Amen to God for his glory"*
2 Corinthians 1:20

Can God do miraculous things today? Yes, just as He did in the days of the early church. We should not say it was just for the Apostles and we cannot expect those things now. God does not often work miracles, but He can if He wants to. Let us give glory to His name that if He does not work miracles, it is because He can and does His will through ordinary methods. He can accomplish what He wants in many ways. Let us never lose heart in such circumstances. He has the same power as He has always had. Many think, if they were living in the days of Elijah, Elisha, or the Apostles, they would expect these things, but because they do not live in those days, they cannot expect to have such answers to prayer. This is wrong. Remember that God has the same power as in the days of the prophets or the Apostles, so let us look for great blessings, and great blessings will be given to us.

Answers to Prayer

May 6, 1845. About six weeks ago, I was told by someone that he expected a certain amount of money and that when he got it, some of it should be given to the Lord. It should be used for the work I was doing, and the other part for Brother Craik's and my own personal expenses.

However, day after day passed and the money did not come. I did not trust in this money, but as it always happened, we were more or less needy, and I thought again and again about this person's promise. However, I did not trust in the one who had made the promise, but in the Lord. Week after week passed and the money did not come. Now, this morning it came to my mind that such promises should not be given too much value—the mind should never be focused on them, but on the living God, and to the living God only. So, I asked the Lord when I was praying with my wife about the work we were doing that He would be pleased to take this whole matter about that promise completely out of my mind and to help me not put any value on it—to treat it as if it was not worth anything, but to keep my eyes directed only on Him. I was enabled to do so.

We had not even finished praying when I received a letter from another person. It was dated May 5, 1845, and it asked about our banking details and whether we could accept a deposit of an amount of money. So, the Lord immediately rewarded this determination not to look at that promise from someone else, but only to Himself.

But, this was not all. At about two o'clock this afternoon, I received a large amount of money from a person who had made that promise over 40 days ago. He had received the money and stayed true to his promise. Some of this money is to be used for the work we are doing, and the remainder for brother Craik's and my own personal expenses.

Feb. 12, 1845. In the morning I met with my dear wife and her sister for prayer to ask the Lord for many blessings in connection with our work, and for the means to do it. About one hour later, I received a letter from Devonshire containing money, some for the orphans, some for a poor brother in Bristol, and some for myself. Besides this proof of the willingness of our Heavenly Father to answer our requests on behalf of the orphans, there is more to be seen.

Praying and Receiving

For many months, the needs of the poor Christians among us have been heavy on my heart. The Bible says, *"For you always have the poor with you, and whenever you want, you can do good for them"* (Mark 14:7). This verse has stirred me again to pray on their behalf, and it was the same today. It was the coldest morning we have had the whole winter. In my morning walk for prayer and meditation, I thought about how well I was supplied with coal, healthy food, and warm clothing, and how many Christians might be in need. I lifted up my heart to God to give me more supplies so that I might be able to have more sympathy for the poor believers in their need through my actions.

It was only three hours later when I received money for myself. And then this evening, an anonymous letter was left at the orphanage containing money for the orphans.

I live in the spirit of prayer—I pray as I walk, when I lie down, and when I rise. And the answers are always coming. Tens of thousands of times my prayers have been answered. When I am persuaded something is right, I go on praying for it until the result comes. I never give up!

Daily Reflections

One of Muller's aims in writing his accounts of managing the orphanages and other work was for Christians like us to be encouraged, inspired, and reminded of God's faithfulness. He is not boasting when he shares about the many times God met the needs of the orphans—he is showing us that it is a reality and it is possible. The record of many answers to prayer is all for our benefit.

1. Does God still perform miracles today?
2. What is your reaction to reading about Muller's many answers he received to prayer?
3. What does it mean to live in the spirit of prayer?
4. Have you received answers to your prayers? What were they? What happened?
5. Read Jeremiah 33:3. What does this verse mean to you?

21

TRUSTING IN HIM FOR ANSWERS

"Commit your way to the LORD;
trust in him, and he will act"
Psalm 37:5

June 15. Today I carried on praying sincerely about the remainder of the money we needed. This evening, an amount was given to make up the shortfall, so now all of it has been received. To the glory of the Lord, whose I am, and whom I serve. Every small coin of this sum of money, and all the pieces of clothing and furniture which I had been praying about, have been given to me, without one single person having been asked by me for anything. The reason why I have chosen not to ask anyone for help is that the hand of God might be clearly seen, that other believers might be encouraged more and more to trust in Him. And also those who do not know the Lord may have fresh proof that it is not a useless thing to pray to God.

As the Lord has chosen, above my expectations, to answer my prayers and to fill my mouth (Psalm 81:10), let us Christians praise Him for His provision. It is a wonderful thing that such a worthless, faithless servant like me should have power with God. Be encouraged for yourselves from this. If someone like me, who is only conformed a little to the mind of Jesus, has his prayers answered, then you also can have your requests given to you.

Over 18 months and 10 days, I have brought this request before God almost every day. From the moment I asked for it until the Lord granted it, I was never allowed to doubt that He would give every coin of that amount of money. Often, I praised Him ahead of time in the confidence that he would grant my request. What we need to look for in prayer is that we believe that we receive, according to Mark 11:24. *"Therefore I tell you, whatever you ask in prayer, believe that you have received it, and it will be yours."*

Isn't it a wonderful thing to trust in the Lord? Isn't a small amount of money from the hands of our Heavenly Father, as the result of having faith in God, wonderful? Won't that attitude cause you to trust in Him and depend on Him for all your everyday concerns, and in all your spiritual matters, too? If you haven't done so, test and try this wonderful way, and you will see how pleasant and good it is. If you have done this to a certain extent, do it even more, and you will never regret it.

But, maybe you are not a believer. You cannot trust in God and go to Him in all circumstances as a Father unless you are first reconciled to him through Jesus. Then what you have to do is learn that you are a lost, ruined, guilty sinner, deserving nothing but punishment. But, at the same time, you have to remember that God, in the greatness of His love for sinners, sent His own Son, that He might bear the punishment they deserve, make an atonement for their sins, and fulfill the law of God in their place so that everyone who believes in Him might have forgiveness of their sins and be made righteous before God.

If you believe in Jesus—if you receive Him as the Son of God (who He is), and the Lamb of God that takes away the sin of the world (what He does), and if you rest on Him, trust in Him for the salvation of your soul—then all your sins shall be forgiven. Even if you have grown old in sin, and you have many terrible sins, the blood of Jesus will clean you from all sin. You must just believe, and you will be saved. And when you are reconciled to God, through faith in His Son, walk before Him as an obedient child, go to God for everything in child-like simplicity, and treat God as your father.

Daily Reflections

Trust forms an important part of our relationship with God. Without it, we cannot depend on Him or believe He will come through for us. It is one thing to pray, but it is quite another to trust He hears, and trust He answers. Many Christians believe in God, believe He is good and has a plan for each one of us, but they do not trust that He has their best interests at heart. We need to trust Him completely if we want to see Him work in our lives.

1. Do you find it easy or difficult to trust God for answers? Why?
2. Read Psalm 37:4-5. What does this verse mean?
3. Why do you think Muller says, "I was never allowed to doubt"?
4. What does it mean to pray to God in child-like simplicity?
5. How does this relate to seeing God as our heavenly Father?

22

PRAYING FOR INTIMACY WITH GOD

Come and hear, all you who fear God,
and I will tell what he has done for my soul.
I cried to him with my mouth,
and high praise was on my tongue.
If I had cherished iniquity in my heart,
the Lord would not have listened.
But truly God has listened;
he has attended to the voice of my prayer
Psalm 66:16-19

Jan. 16, Tuesday. A wonderful day. How good is the Lord! Enthusiasm in my spirit has been given to me through His grace this morning. If it was not for God's help, I should have lost it again.

The weather has been very cold for several days, but today I suffered a lot, either because it was colder than before or because I felt it more due to the weakness of my body, and having taken so much medicine. I got up from my knees and stoked the fire, but I was still very cold. I was a little irritated by this. I moved to another part of the room but felt the cold even more. At last, having prayed for some time, I was compelled to get up and take a walk to increase blood circulation in my body.

I now begged the Lord on my walk that this circumstance might not rob me of the precious intimacy which I have had with Him for the last three days. This was what Satan was aiming to do. I also confessed my sin of irritability because of the cold and looked to have my conscience cleansed through the blood of Jesus. He had mercy on me, my peace was restored, and when I returned, I continued in prayer and had uninterrupted intimacy with Him. I have mentioned this circumstance on purpose to show how the most insignificant causes can suddenly rob us of the enjoyment of the most wonderful intimacy with God.

I have been able to pray for several hours today. The subject of my meditation has been Psalm 66, and these verses have been especially appropriate to what I am going through. God has already, through using my illness, brought me into *"a place of abundance"* (v. 12), and I believe He will still bless my soul even more.

I do not remember another moment when I had more passion in my spirit to overcome everything wrong in the sight of God, and with such sincerity to be fully conformed to the image of Jesus. For this I can apply verse 16 to myself, and *"tell what he has done for my soul"*—I can also take verse 18 for myself. I do not allow iniquity in my heart, but it is pure before Him, through His grace, and therefore God does hear my prayers.

Many things have been put on my heart in prayer, especially that the Lord would create in me a holy passion to win souls and greater compassion for lost sinners.

Daily Reflections

Although we are spiritual beings, we live most of the time in our emotions, surrounded by physical circumstances, and dealing with mental issues. It's not often that we find ourselves in moments where we are so connected with God that the words communion and intimacy become real to us. When we do have those times, we hang on to them, hoping they will last before the next worldly concern snaps us out of it. Prayer is one of the places where we can find these moments.

1. What does it mean to have an intimate moment with God?
2. How can we enter into this communion with the Lord?
3. Read James 4:8. What does this verse mean?
4. What things rob you of having these moments of experiencing deep personal time with Jesus?
5. What is the benefit of having intimate moments with God?

23

FAITH IN PRAYING FOR THE SICK

"And the prayer of faith will save the one who is sick,
and the Lord will raise him up"
James 5:15

February 18. This afternoon I broke a blood vessel in my stomach and lost a lot of blood.

February 19. This morning, on Sunday, I was called on to be at the chapel today, as it involved four villages, where some had been preaching because I was not able to do so, and one of them would need to stay at home to take my place. I asked them to come back in about an hour when I would give them an answer. After they were gone, the Lord gave me the faith to get up. I dressed and decided to go to the chapel. I was enabled to do so, even though I was very weak. The short walk to the chapel was a huge effort for me. I was enabled to preach this morning with my normal loud, strong voice, and for the normal amount of time.

After the morning meeting, a doctor friend begged me not to preach again in the afternoon, as it might cause me even more injury. I told him that it would be very arrogant to do this unless the Lord gave me faith. I did preach in the afternoon, and this doctor called again and said the same about the evening meeting. But, having faith, I preached again in the evening. After each meeting, I became stronger, which was clear proof that the hand of God was working. After the third meeting, I immediately went to bed, realizing that it would be arrogant to needlessly test my strength.

February 20. The Lord enabled me to get up early in the morning and to go to our usual prayer meeting where I read, spoke, and prayed. Afterward, I wrote four letters, shared about the Bible at home, and attended the meeting again in the evening.

February 21. I attended the two meetings as usual, preached in the evening, and did all my other work as well.

February 22. Today I attended the meeting in the morning, then walked six miles with two Christians to Newton Bushel, and rode from there to Plymouth.

February 23. I am now as well as I was before I broke the blood vessel.

In sharing the details of this circumstance, I want to warn everyone who reads this not to copy me in this way if they have no faith. But if you do have faith, it will be honored by God. I could not say that if this happened again, I would act in the same way, because when I was not as weak as when I had broken the blood vessel and had no faith, I did not preach. But, if it pleases the Lord to give me faith, I might be able to do the same, even though I will be weak.

About this time I repeatedly prayed with sick believers until they were healed. Unconditionally, I asked the Lord for the blessing of physical health, and almost always it was granted. In some instances, however, the prayer was not answered. While in London, Nov. 1829, in answer to my prayers, I was immediately restored from a physical sickness which I had been struggling with for a long time, and which has never come back again since.

The way in which I can explain these facts is: It pleased the Lord to give me something like the gift (not grace) of faith, so that unconditionally, I could ask and look for an answer. The difference between the gift and the grace of faith is this: According to the *gift* of faith, I am able to do something, or believe that something will come to pass—not doing it or not believing it would not be sin. According to the *grace* of faith I am able to do something, or believe something will happen according to the Bible as proof, and therefore, not doing it, or not believing it would be sin.

For example, the gift of faith is necessary to believe that a sick person should be healed again though there is no human probability—there is no promise to that effect. The grace of faith is needed to believe that the Lord will give me what I need to live, if I first seek the kingdom of God and His righteousness—there is a promise to that effect (Matt. 6:33).

Daily Reflections

In Jesus' time of ministry on earth, he healed countless people and also gave his disciples the power to do the same. Healing is something we believe God can and will do, but we all have different views on how and when. When nothing happens, we have many reasons and excuses, but the fact remains that if we pray, God can and does heal! Muller's account is honest and straightforward, admitting he did not always see results, but he continued in faith.

1. Do you believe God can still heal people today?
2. Have you ever been physically healed after prayer from a certain sickness or ailment?
3. Read Psalm 30:2. What does this verse mean?
4. Why is faith so important when it comes to praying for healing?
5. What is the difference between the grace and the gift of faith?

24

WAITING FOR ANSWERS

*"Ask, and it will be given to you; seek, and you will find;
knock, and it will be opened to you.
For everyone who asks receives, and the one who seeks finds, and to the
one who knocks it will be opened"*
Matthew 7:7-8

Nothing is said in the verse about the time and manner in which your prayer is to be answered. *"Ask, and it will be given to you."* There is a positive promise, but nothing about time. *"Seek, and you will find; knock, and it will be opened to you."* We have to patiently and quietly continue waiting on God until the blessing is given. Someone might say, "Must I bring a matter before God two, three, five, or even twenty times? Is it not enough to tell Him once?" We might as well say there is no need to tell Him once, because He already knows what our need is. He wants us to prove that we have confidence in Him, that we take our place as creatures before the Creator.

Why We Wait

Also, we must not forget that there may be reasons why prayer is not immediately answered. One reason may be the need for the exercise of our faith, because faith is strengthened in exercising it. By the trial, it is strengthened. Another reason may be to glorify God by showing patience. There may be another reason. Our heart may not yet be prepared for the answer to our prayer. Christians must wait, but when the heart is ready for the blessing, it will be given. Many Christians struggle because prayer is not immediately answered. Because the prayer remains unanswered for weeks or years, they stop asking God and lose the blessing they would have obtained if they persevered.

Immediate and Delayed Answers

While some of us receive the blessing very soon, others have to wait for many years. I have had immediate answers to prayer. Often, before leaving my bedroom, I had an answer to a prayer I gave that same morning, and during the day I have had five or six more answers to prayer. But not all of them have been answered immediately. Sometimes I have had to wait weeks, months, or years. I heard about the conversion of six people I had been praying for, one of them I had been praying for, for over two and three years; another between three and four years; the fifth about fifteen years; and the sixth over twenty years. I once asked something from God, and even though I brought it every day before Him, in confidence, thanking Him for the answer before it was received, I still had to wait three years before the blessing was given to me. Another time I had to wait six years. I once brought a matter about twenty thousand times before God, with full assurance of faith, and yet eleven and a half years passed before the answer was given.

At one time my faith was tested even more than this. In November 1844, I began to pray for the conversion of five individuals. I prayed every day, whether I was sick or healthy, on the land or on the sea, and whatever business engagements I had. Eighteen months went by before the first one was converted. I thanked God and continued praying for the others. Five years went by, and then the second one was born again. I thanked God, and prayed on for the other three. Every day I continued to pray for them, and six more years passed before the third was converted. I thanked God and went on praying for the other two. These two remain unconverted. I have been praying every day for nearly 36 years for these two individuals, and yet they remain unconverted. But I hope in God, I pray on, and look yet for the answer.

[One of these was converted before Muller's death, and the other only after Müller had died.]

See that the help never comes too late. We may be poor, but the help comes at the right time. We may have to wait on the Lord for a long time, but at last He helps. It may seem as if the Lord had forgotten us by allowing us to be poor week after week, but eventually He helps abundantly. He shows that it is only for the trial of our faith, for our own benefit and the benefit of those who might hear of His dealings with us, that He made us pray so long to Him.

So, carry on waiting on God, go on praying. Just be sure you ask for things which are according to the will of God. The conversion of sinners is in line with His will, because He does not want the death of the sinner. This God has revealed to us in 2 Peter 3:9 that He does not wish *"that any should perish, but that all should reach repentance."* Continue praying, expect an answer, look for it, and in the end you will have to praise God for it.

Daily Reflections

God always answers, but sometimes He takes His time doing so. This can be frustrating for us, especially when we have our own ideas of the time frame we expect Him to come through. Waiting is one of the hardest things we as humans have to do, and it's one of the things God asks us to do most often! Muller is very practical and open about how some answers come instantaneously and some might take time, but he encourages us to continue waiting.

1. Why does Muller say God wants us to ask Him more than once about certain things?
2. What are the reasons why we must wait?
3. Why is praying for sinners to get saved one of the prayers God will answer?
4. Are you persistent in your prayers or not?

25

THE POWER OF PRAYING TOGETHER

"Again I say to you, if two of you agree on earth about anything they ask, it will be done for them by my Father in heaven"
Matthew 18:19

"So Peter was kept in prison, but earnest prayer for him was made to God by the church" (Acts 12:5). See here, we have prayer in church capacity. The saints at Jerusalem meeting together and giving themselves to prayer. *"When he realized this, he went to the house of Mary, the mother of John whose other name was Mark, where many were gathered together and were praying"* (Acts 12:12). Notice that *"many were gathered together and were praying."* Prayer was made by the church on his behalf without ceasing. Though it was the night before his execution, they did not lose heart. Though the case seems hopeless, they still come together to pray. Therefore, they had not only begun well, but they had also gone on well; they had continued in prayer.

There is one point I want to emphasize and encourage all Christians on, and that is united prayer. The Lord Jesus says, *"Again I say to you, if two of you agree on earth about anything they ask, it will be done for them by my Father in heaven."* So, if there are Christians who have relatives who are not born again yet, and if they could join with two or more other people and collectively ask God to convert their children, then will the blessing not come in this way?

They should plead this promise before the Lord, read it out when they meet, and put their finger—so to speak—on it. If they meet once a week for half an hour, or once every two weeks, or as often as they can to plead this promise before the Lord, after a while a father would be able to say, "My son, who almost broke my heart, has been converted," and a mother could say, "I have a letter from my daughter, who left my home 15 years ago and has been living in sin, telling me she has found Jesus."

Their faith would be strengthened by such united prayer and such testimonies! After a while, as their faith became stronger, they would collectively pray for their pastor, that God would bless his work in reaching and converting the lost more, and in blessing the church. And as they became stronger and larger in their prayers, it would extend to praying for the missions and the spreading of the gospel. They would know the power and wonder of prayer more and more abundantly and would sincerely wait on God, asking Him again and again to bring a mighty revival in the church as a whole, worldwide.

If this happened, imagine what power ministers would go out with to share the truth of the gospel, what blessings would come on our Sunday Schools, on giving out Bibles, on open-air preaching, and other Christian work. God help us to give ourselves to prayer even more passionately and sincerely!

The spiritual condition of the orphans under our care caused us great sadness in our hearts, because there were so few among them who were serious about their souls, resting on the atoning death of Jesus for their salvation. This led us to ask the whole staff of assistants, matrons, and teachers to earnestly seek the Lord's blessing on the children's souls. This was done in our united prayer meetings, and I believe it continued in secret prayer as well. In answer to these secret and united prayers, in the year 1872, there were more believers by far among the orphans than ever.

Daily Reflections

Although Christianity is a personal walk with Jesus, it's not meant to be done all on our own. Fellowship is a key aspect. Bringing petitions to God on our own, in secret, is one of the highest callings, but there is also incredible power in coming together and agreeing in prayer. Unity is in the heart of God —Father, Son, and Holy Spirit. It's why He calls us to link spiritually with other Christians, so His will can be shown through us as brothers and sisters.

1. Have you ever noticed a difference between praying on your own and praying together with others?

2. Does your church have prayer meetings? Do you attend them?
3. Read 1 Corinthians 1:10. Why is Paul so adamant on this point?
4. How is faith strengthened by united prayer?
5. Why is the Trinity such an important part of our Christian doctrine?

26

FINDING THE WILL OF GOD

"Do not be conformed to this world,
but be transformed by the renewal of your mind,
that by testing you may discern what is the will of God,
what is good and acceptable and perfect"
Romans 12:2

How important it is to ascertain the will of God before we do anything, because then we are not only blessed in our own souls, but also the work of our hands will prosper.

The more things we do according to the will of God, the more we are blessed and made a blessing. Our manner of living is according to the mind of the Lord, for He delights in seeing His children come to Him in this way.

We do not have to rush forward in our own self-will and say, "I will do the work, and I will trust the Lord for means," because this cannot be real trust—it is the counterfeit of faith, it is presumption. Even though God, in His mercy, may eventually help us out of debt or trouble, this does not prove that we were right in going forward before it was His time to do so. We should rather say to ourselves: "Am I actually doing the work of God?"

And if so, I may not be the person to do it. Or, if I am the person, His time may not yet be right for me to go forward. It may be His good pleasure to exercise my faith and patience. I should, therefore, quietly wait for His time, because when it comes, God will help. Acting on this principle brings blessing.

At the beginning, I get my heart into such a state that it has no will of its own in regard to the matter. Nine-tenths of the trouble with people is right here. Nine-tenths of the difficulties are overcome when our hearts are ready to do the Lord's will, whatever it may be. When one is truly in this state, it is usually not far from finding the knowledge of what His will is.

Having done this, I do not leave the result to how I feel in my emotions. If I do so, I leave myself open to being distracted and deluded.

I seek the will of the Spirit of God through, or in connection with, the Word of God. The Spirit and the Word must be combined. If I look to the Spirit alone without the Word, I also leave myself open to misinterpretation. If the Holy Spirit guides us at all, He will do it according to the Scriptures and never contrary to them.

Next, I take into account favorable circumstances. These often clearly indicate God's will in connection with His Word and Spirit.

I ask God in prayer to reveal His will to me clearly and correctly.

So, *through prayer* to God, the study of the Bible, and reflection, I come to judge according to the best of my ability and knowledge, and if my mind is at peace and continues like this after two or three more requests, I proceed accordingly. In small matters, and in transactions involving the most important issues, I have found this method always effective.

To find out the Lord's will, we should always use scriptural means. Prayer, the Bible, and His Spirit should be united together. We should go to the Lord repeatedly in prayer and ask Him to teach us by His Spirit through His word. I say by His Spirit through His word because if we should think that His Spirit led us to do something, due to certain facts being as they are, but His Word is opposed to the step which we are going to take, we are deceiving ourselves. No situation, no business will be given to me by God in which I do not have enough time to care about my soul. Therefore, whatever the outward circumstances might look like, it can only be considered as allowed by God to prove the genuineness of my love, faith, and obedience, but not as the leading of His provision to tempt me to act contrary to His revealed will.

Daily Reflections

Probably one of the most asked questions is, "What is the will of God?" Many Christians spend their whole lives trying to find the answer, often searching through the Scriptures and asking advice from lots of people without ever coming close to what the plan of the Lord is. His will is not a huge mystery that He purposely made difficult for us to understand. It's denying ourselves and doing what He asks of us, following the example Jesus set for us while he was on earth.

1. What do you understand as the will of God for your own life?
2. Read Romans 12:2. What does this verse mean?
3. Why is waiting for God so important when it comes to knowing the will of God?
4. What three things are needed to know God's will?
5. What is self-denial? Read Matthew 16:24.

27

EFFECTIVE PRAYER

"The prayer of a righteous person has great power as it is working"
James 5:16

F ive conditions necessary for effective, successful prayer:

1- Entire dependence on the merits and mediation of Jesus as the only ground for any claim for blessing.

"Whatever you ask in my name, that I will do, so that the Father may be glorified in the Son. If you ask me anything in my name, I will do it" (John 14:13-14).

Jesus said we should ask in His name if we want our requests to be granted (John 14:13-14). Experienced Christians should know what it means to ask in the name of Jesus, but we have to ask in union with Christ, as members of the body of which He is the Head. We stand before God in the righteousness of Christ; we are justified by faith in His name, and therefore, we come before God as those who are one with Him.

We put Jesus forward, and we put ourselves in the background. We are entirely unworthy of receiving one blessing from the hand of God. Ask God to show you that all you deserve is hell and torment. This is the only thing that we have merited. We deserve nothing else; and therefore, all we receive (out of hell) must come in the name of Jesus.

We are not only permitted but commanded to come in the name of Jesus. I have been made clean by the power of the blood of Jesus. I deserve nothing but punishment, but Jesus Christ is worthy to receive the choicest of the blessings which God has to give. Therefore, if I put myself in the background, put Jesus forward, and in His name ask the best of God's blessings, they are granted to me.

It is very important that we understand this. Do we habitually plead the worth of Jesus when we come before God with our requests?

2- Separation from all known sin.

If we allow iniquity in our hearts, the Lord will not hear us, for that would be allowing sin. *"If I had cherished iniquity in my heart, the LORD would not have listened"* (Psalm 66:18). If we are left to ourselves and forsake the Lord, trusting in our flesh, or we allow sin in our heart (willfully and habitually doing anything against the will of God), then we can pray and say many words before Him, but He will not hear us.

3- Faith in God's promise, confirmed by His oath.

Not to believe Him is to make Him a liar. *"And without faith it is impossible to please him, for whoever would draw near to God must believe that he exists and that he rewards those who seek him"* (Heb. 11:6).

We have to exercise faith in the power of God, and in the love and willingness of God to grant us our requests. And this is made a condition in this verse. We must be looking out for the answer. There are few Christians who doubt His ability to give, but many doubt His willingness, forgetting what Paul said: *"He who did not spare his own Son but gave him up for us all, how will he not also with him graciously give us all things?"* (Romans 8:32). It was in grace that He gave His Son for us. So, He is, in grace, willing to give us everything that will be for our good. What more do we need than this?

4- Asking in accordance with His will.

Our motives must be godly: We must not seek any gift of God to use it on our lusts. *"And this is the confidence that we have toward him, that if we ask anything according to his will he hears us"* (1 John 5:14). *"You ask and do not receive, because you ask wrongly, to spend it on your passions"* (James 4:3).

If we want our requests to be answered, we have to ask God for things that are according to His will. We cannot expect an answer that goes against His will. If we want to know a little of the will of God about any matter, the first thing is to ask Him to teach us and instruct us. We can also ask for help from other Christians. But we must ask for things according to the will of God, because He loves us with an infinitely wise love, and not like foolish parents who give their children everything they ask for. He desires true, real happiness and blessing for His children, and only gives what would be for our blessing and profit.

5- Persistence in supplication.

There must be waiting on God and waiting for God, as the farmer has long patience to wait for the harvest. *"Be patient, therefore, brothers, until the coming of the Lord. See how the farmer waits for the precious fruit of the earth, being patient about it, until it receives the early and the late rains"* (James 5:7).

Daily Reflections

We all want our prayers to be effective and powerful; otherwise, what's the use of praying? But most of us end up being content with saying a few lines in the hope that they might get through to heaven. Instead of being filled with faith, they're packed with desperation. But here, Muller lays out five conditions that, if followed, will guarantee us life-changing prayers that God will act on.

1. Why is praying in Jesus' name so important to prayer?
2. Muller repeats the second condition a few times in his writings. Why is it critical to have our prayers heard?
3. How do we exercise faith in God's promises?

4. How do we find out what the will of God is so we can pray in line with it?
5. Read Psalm 37 and see how many times it speaks about waiting. Why does God expect us to wait so often for Him?

28

PRAYING TO SHARE THE WORD

*"If any of you lacks wisdom, let him ask God,
who gives generously to all without reproach,
and it will be given him"*
James 1:5

I have found the best method of preparation for preaching the Word that comes from deep conviction, and from experiencing God's blessing on it, for my own enjoyment, the benefit of Christians, and the conversion of sinners, is as follows:

I do not presume to know what is best for the congregation, and I, therefore, ask the Lord in the first place, that He would teach me on what subject I shall speak, or what portion of His Word I will present. Now, sometimes it happens that before I ask Him, a subject or passage has been in my mind which seems good to speak on. In that case, I ask the Lord whether I should speak on this subject or passage. If, after prayer, I am persuaded on it, I still leave myself open to the Lord to change it if He wants.

Frequently, however, I have no verse or subject in my mind before I give myself to prayer to find the Lord's will concerning it. In this case, I wait some time on my knees for an answer, trying to listen to the voice of the Spirit to direct me. If a passage or subject is brought to my mind while I am on my knees, or after I have finished praying, I again ask the Lord whether it is His will that I should speak on that. Sometimes I ask repeatedly, especially if the subject or verse is not a common one. If after prayer, my mind is peaceful about it, I take this to be the verse but still leave myself open to the Lord for direction, if He chooses to change it, or if I have been mistaken.

Frequently, it happens that I have no verse or subject on my mind before praying for guidance, but I also do not get one after praying once, or twice, or more times about it. At first, I used to be very confused when this happened but now for more than 45 years, the Lord has given me peace about it. What I do is to go on with my regular reading of the Scriptures, praying (while I read) for a verse, every now and then putting my Bible down for prayer until I get one. Sometimes, I have had to read five, ten, or twenty chapters before the Lord gave me a verse. Many times I have even had to go to the meeting without one and obtained it only a few minutes before I was going to speak. But, I have never lacked the Lord's assistance at the time of preaching, provided I had sincerely sought it in private.

The preacher cannot know the particular state of the various individuals who are in the congregation, nor what they require, but the Lord knows. If the preacher leaves his own wisdom aside, he will be assisted by the Lord, but if he chooses his own wisdom, then he should not be surprised if he sees little benefit or result from his efforts.

Daily Reflections

Many of us may never share from behind the pulpit in church, but we will all have the opportunity at some point to speak to others. It may be one-on-one or in a small group. Regardless, we need the Word of God in our hearts so that what we say is not of ourselves but of the Lord. Preparation is important, whether we are pastors, in the ministry, or part of a congregation, and prayer is the way to do this.

1. Have you ever had to share the Gospel without warning? What happened?
2. What is the difference between sharing your own words and sharing in the spirit?
3. Read Luke 12:12. If the Holy Spirit gives us the words to say, do we still need to prepare?
4. Why does God use us humans as His voice to the world rather than speaking audibly from heaven?
5. Is it more important for a pastor to prepare than for a member of the congregation?

29

PRAYING TO SHARE THE WORD (CONTINUED)

"The Holy Spirit will teach you in that very hour what you ought to say"
Luke 12:12

Now, when the verse has been obtained, whether it is one or two or more verses, or a whole chapter or more, I ask the Lord that He would teach me by His Holy Spirit, while I meditate over it. Within the last 50 years, I have found it the most beneficial to meditate with my pen in my hand, writing down the outlines as the Word is opened to me. I do not do this to memorize them, or as if what I wrote was the only words I would say, but for the sake of clarity to help me see how far I understand the passage.

I also find it useful afterward to refer to what I have written. I seldom use any other help besides the little I understand of the original of the Scriptures and some good translations in other languages. My main help is prayer. I have *never* in my life begun to study one single part of divine truth without gaining some light about it, when I have been able really to give myself to prayer and meditation over it. I have often found it difficult, partly because of my own weakness, and partly due to sickness and other engagements. I strongly believe that no one should expect to see any good coming from his efforts in word and doctrine if he does not pray and meditate.

Having prayed and meditated on the subject or verse, I leave myself completely in the hands of the Lord. I ask Him to bring to my mind what I have seen in my room concerning the subject I am going to speak on, which He often does, and teaches me much more while I am preaching.

There is, however, a way to prepare for the preaching of the Word which is even better than the one I have spoken of. It is this: to live in such constant and real communion with the Lord, and to be so habitually and frequently in meditation over the truth, that even without the points I have made, we have obtained food for others and know the mind of the Lord about the subject or the portion of the Word on which we should speak. But I have only experienced this in a small way, though I long to be brought into such a state that habitually *"out of his heart will flow rivers of living water"* (John 7:38).

Daily Reflections

If you have been working through these reflections on your own, why not share what you've learned or discovered with someone else? It's always good to be encouraged and even challenged. This is one of the ways we grow and mature in our knowledge of the Bible and of the things of God. Share with someone you trust from church, not just anybody. Make sure they are also grounded in their faith and understanding of the Gospel. This will ensure you have a solid sounding board.

1. What does it mean to share your testimony?
2. Read Romans 10:14. Is this verse only for pastors?
3. Read Acts 1:8. Was this verse only for Jesus' disciples, or do you think it pertains to us today?
4. When last did you share the Gospel with someone who is not a Christian?
5. Why is it important to pray before, during, and after we share about Jesus?

30

IN EVERYTHING BY PRAYER

"Do not be anxious about anything, *but in everything by prayer and supplication with thanksgiving let your requests be made known to God*"
Philippians 4:6

You might read the Bible and seem to understand it well, but if you are not in the habit of always waiting on God, you will make little progress in your spiritual life. Naturally, there is nothing good in any of us, and so we cannot expect to please Him, except by His help.

Jesus gave us an example about this in his own life. He gave entire nights to prayer. We see Him on the lonely mountain at night engaged in prayer. And just as He is to be an example to us in everything, it is especially true on this point. He is an example to us. The old evil, corrupt nature is still in us, even though we are born again, so we have to come in prayer to God for help. We have to hold onto the power of the Mighty One. For everything, we have to pray. Not just when huge trouble comes, when the house is on fire, or a wife is close to dying, or the children are sick—not just in these times, but also in little things. From the very early morning, let us make everything a matter of prayer, and let it be like this throughout the day, and throughout our whole life.

A Christian lady once said that she heard me speak on this subject 35 years ago, and that I referred to praying about little things. She reminded me that I had told everyone to imagine a parcel arrived, but it was very difficult to untie the knot, and it could not be cut. I said we should ask God to help in that moment, even to untie the knot. I had forgotten saying those words, but she remembered them, and she said that they had been a great help to her again and again.

So I would say to you, there is nothing too little to pray about. In the simplest things connected with our daily life and walk, we should give ourselves to prayer. If we do this, we will have the living, loving Lord Jesus to help us. Even in the most insignificant matters I pray in the morning, and before I leave my room, I often have two or three answers to prayer by doing this.

In the spiritual life in your souls, learn, in childlike simplicity, to wait on God for everything! Treat the Lord Jesus Christ as your personal friend, able and willing to help you in everything. What a blessing it is to be carried in His loving arms all the day long! I would say that the spiritual life of the believer is made up of a huge number of little circumstances and little things. Every day, there are a number of little trials, and if we try to deal with them in our own strength and wisdom, we will quickly find that we are confused. But if we take everything to God, we shall be helped, and our way shall be made clear and simple. In this way, our life will be a happy life!

I want to encourage you with this verse for the benefit of your hearts: *"In everything by prayer and supplication with thanksgiving let your requests be made known to God."* That means not just when the trial is incredibly huge, that we must only pray then, but about little things, the ordinary affairs of life—to bring them all before God. And the result of this is that *"the peace of God, which surpasses all understanding, will guard your hearts and your minds in Christ Jesus"* (Phil. 4:7). Though this is a tough life filled with suffering, we are able to cheerfully go through the world. It is my habitual practice to bring little things before God. I never attempt to carry any burdens myself. I bring them to God and speak to Him about them. The first thing when we meet every morning is to have prayer about all of our work, and to bring everything before our God. The smallest things we bring before God, hand them over to Him, and do not try to carry them ourselves.

Daily Reflections

Often we wait until we are in desperate need before we turn to God in anxiety, begging Him to come through for us. Muller brought everything before the Lord; whether it was food, finances, or faith, he asked the Lord to provide. This was at the core of his lifestyle, to ask for everything, no matter how big or how small it was. He was not worried about hassling God. He believed there was no provider but God, even if the provision came through other means.

1. Do you ask God for things? What types of things do you ask for?
2. Read Matthew 6:8. Why do we have to ask if God already knows what we need?
3. Do you experience the peace spoken of in Philippians 4:7 once you have brought your requests to God?
4. What are the needs in your life right at this moment?
5. Read Philippians 4:19. What does this verse mean to you?

31

CONFIDING IN GOD

"Trust in him at all times, O people;
pour out your heart before him;
God is a refuge for us"
Psalm 62:8

God wants to increase the faith of Christians. Our weak faith is developed and strengthened more and more by use. Instead of not wanting trials before victory, not exercising patience, we should be willing to take them from God's hand as the food of faith. When we ask to have our faith strengthened, we must be willing to accept the way God gives us to strengthen it. We must allow Him to educate us through trials, sorrow, and troubles. It is through trials that faith is exercised and developed more and more. God allows difficulties so that He may develop what He is willing to do for us.

In the darkest moments, I am able to confide in Him, because I know how beautiful, kind, and loving He is. If it is the will of God to put us in the furnace, let Him do it so that we may know Him more as He reveals Himself. If this is the attitude of our hearts, we can say, "It is my Father, let Him do as He pleases."

When I first began to allow God to deal with me, relying on Him, taking Him at His word, starting 50 years ago to rely on Him for myself, family, taxes, traveling expenses, and every other need, I rested on the simple promises I found in the sixth chapter of Matthew. I believed the Word, I rested on it and practiced it. I took God at His Word.

A foreigner in England, I knew seven languages and might have been able to use them as a way to find employment, but I had set myself apart to work for the Lord. I relied on the God who has promised, and He has acted according to His Word. I've lacked nothing—nothing. I have had trials and difficulties, and had an empty wallet, but the books have always balanced in the end. I have received thousands and thousands of dollars over the last 51 years. There will always be difficulties, always trials. But God has sustained me through them, and the work has gone on.

Now, this is not because I am a person of great mental power, or I have lots of energy and perseverance—these are not the reasons. It is because I have confided in God; because I have sought God, and He has cared for the orphanages, schools, and everyone involved.

I do not carry the burden. At 67 years old, I have the physical strength and mental sharpness for as much work as when I was a young man in university studying. How is that possible? Because in the last 50 years of work, I've been able to rely on God with the simplicity of a child. I have had my trials, but I have laid hold of God, and so I have been sustained. It is not only permission but positive command that He tells us to cast our burdens on Him. Let us do this! Brothers and sisters in Christ, *"Cast your burden on the LORD, and he will sustain you"* (Psalm 55:22). Every day I do it. This morning, I brought 60 matters before the Lord regarding the church where I am pastor, and this is the way I do it every day, year by year; 10 years, 30 years, 40 years.

Do not expect to immediately have full faith. Keep your heart in the Word of God and your faith will increase as you exercise it. Some say, "Oh, I shall never have the gift of faith Mr. Muller has got." This is a mistake. My faith is the same kind of faith that all Christians have had. It is the same kind that Simon Peter had, and all Christians may obtain the like faith. My faith is their faith, though there may be more of it because my faith has been a little more developed by exercise than theirs.

Start small. At first, I was able to trust the Lord for ten dollars, then for a hundred dollars, then for a thousand dollars, and now, with the greatest ease, I could trust Him for a million dollars if I had to. But first, I must quietly, carefully, deliberately examine and see whether what I was trusting for was something in accordance with His promises in His written Word.

Daily Reflections

There is always more to learn about God. Not even the greatest professors of theology or the most mature Christian can know everything. It's why we all need the Holy Spirit. It's why we all need to spend time in the Bible and in prayer. God wants to reveal more and more of himself to us. If you have worked through these reflections and been open, then God will teach you how to pray, how to have faith in prayer, and how you can also have faith just like Muller did.

1. What does "confiding in God" mean for you?
2. Do you ever bring things to God that may seem inconsequential when it comes to spiritual matters?
3. Are there people of great faith in your church, community, or your life you can look up to as examples?
4. How does our faith grow according to Muller?
5. After reading this book and working through these reflections, have you grown in your prayer life, in your understanding of prayer?

MORE ON PRAYER

Perhaps you want to learn more about prayer and how you can also be effective when you come before God with your petitions. There are other Christians like George Muller who are esteemed and regarded as inspirational in what they have written about prayer. Reading these books by classic authors and working through the reflections will open your spiritual eyes to see more:

- E.M. Bounds on Prayer: *31 Life-Changing Insights from EM Bounds on How to Pray with Daily Reflections*
- J.C. Ryle on Prayer: *31 Insights for Understanding the Purpose and Power of Prayer*
- C.H. Spurgeon on Prayer: *31 Effective Insights on How to Pray with Daily Reflections*
- John Bunyan on Prayer: *31 Biblical Insights for Effective Prayer*

ABOUT GEORGE MULLER

In 1805, George Muller was born in a village called Kroppenstadt in Prussia (now Germany). He grew up with his brother having everything they needed supplied by their father, a revenue collector working for the government. Despite being given more than enough money, the young Muller stole, lied, and had no conscience of his actions.

When he was 10 years old, he was sent to the cathedral school in Halberstadt. His father, not being a religious man at all, was not concerned about him serving God but hoped his son might earn a comfortable living off the State Church.

Muller was 14 when his mother died, but he was too busy playing cards and drinking with his friends to show any care. His lying, gambling, and stealing grew worse after that, even during his confirmation service, when he cheated the priest out of money. He continued to steal from his father, living in "much sin." By the age of 16, he found himself in prison after trying to con his way out of paying for a room at an inn.

After being severely disciplined by his father, he ended up going to a school in Nordhausen where he displayed incredible intellect and diligence in his studies. He moved to the University of Halle, where he continued his life of lying, stealing, and living in pleasure, even though he was now qualified to preach.

In 1825, he attended a prayer meeting which had such an impact on the young man that he began to change his lifestyle. Seeing a man kneeling down and praying, Muller was convinced he needed salvation and soon was born again. He now wanted to become a missionary, something which his father would not allow. Muller realized he could no longer accept the money he had been receiving from home, and God began to make a way for him to complete his studies.

In 1829, he moved to England as a missionary to the Jews but became very sick and was sent to Teignmouth to recuperate. Here, he met Henry Craik, a man who would become his lifelong friend and colleague in the work amongst orphans. He became the pastor of Ebenezer Chapel and soon married Miss Mary Groves. But his heart had been stirred for the lost, the poor, and those without parents. He gave up his salary and began to trust the lord to meet his needs.

In 1832, he moved to Bethesda Chapel with Craik, where they would remain while devoted to all his other work. He opened up day schools where boys and girls could be supported and taught, and in 1836 transformed the house he was in to become the first of many orphanages. By 1845, the noise and number of children meant they had to look for new premises, and four years later a new building was constructed, paid for without Muller ever borrowing or asking for any money. It was one of his principles to rely completely on the Lord for everything, never making his needs public. Through a life of daily prayer, Muller trusted

God to supply all the needs of five orphanages that housed almost 2,000 children.

In 1875, Muller began traveling across the globe, visiting India, America, New Zealand, and much of Europe among many other countries, spreading the gospel and preaching wherever he went. Even then, he relied on God to cover all his costs! He continued these evangelistic tours until he was 90 years old.

Muller died on 10 March 1898. In his lifetime, he cared for over 10,000 orphans and provided education to about 120,000 children through his schools. He saw his life as a testimony more than anything else. Everything he did, and everything the Lord provided, was an example and proof that God is faithful.

"The greater the difficulty to be overcome, the more will it be seen to the glory of God how much can be done by prayer and faith."

BIBLIOGRAPHY

Crossway. (2001). *English Standard Version Bible*. Crossway Bibles.
Muller, G. (2011). *An Hour with George Muller*. Literary Licensing, LLC.
Muller, G. (2015). *George Muller's Sermons and Addresses*. CreateSpace.
Muller, G. (2018). *Answers to Prayer*. Lulu.com. www.GeorgeMuller.org
Müller, G. (2022). *A Narrative of Some of the Lord's Dealings With George Müller (The Complete Four-Volume Edition)*. DigiCat.
Muller, G., Bergin, G. F., & Pierson, A. T. (1905). *Autobiography of George Müller, compiled by G. Fred. Bergin*. London, Bristol.
Murray, A. (2019). *George Muller and the Secret of His Power in Prayer*. Amazon Digital Services LLC - KDP Print US.
Ross, S. (2022). *Real Faith by George Muller - Christian Biography Resources*. Www.wholesomewords.org. https://www.wholesomewords.org/etexts/muller/faith.html
Sarkis, P. (2019). *A Quiet Time with George Müller*. Lulu.com.
Thomas Nelson Publishers. (2014). *Holy Bible, KJV*. Thomas Nelson Pub.

www.ingramcontent.com/pod-product-compliance
Lightning Source LLC
LaVergne TN
LVHW021239080526
838199LV00088B/4793